Also by Lidia Matticchio Bastianich

Lidia's Italy in America

Nonna Tell Me a Story: Lidia's Christmas Kitchen

Lidia Cooks from the Heart of Italy

Lidia's Italy

Lidia's Family Table

Lidia's Italian-American Kitchen

Lidia's Italian Table

La Cucina di Lidia

LIDIA'S FAVORITE RECIPES

LIDIA'S
FAVORITE RECIPES

100 Foolproof Italian Dishes,
from Basic Sauces to Irresistible Entrées

LIDIA MATTICCHIO BASTIANICH
and TANYA BASTIANICH MANUALI

Photographs by Marcus Nilsson

Alfred A. Knopf   New York   2012

This Is a Borzoi Book
Published by Alfred A. Knopf

www.aaknopf.com

Knopf, Borzoi Books, and the colophon are registered trademarks of Random House, Inc.

Library of Congress Cataloging-in-Publication Data

Bastianich, Lidia.
Lidia's favorite recipes : 100 foolproof Italian dishes, from basic sauces to irresistible entrées / by
Lidia Matticchio Bastianich and Tanya Bastianich Manuali ; photographs by Marcus Nilsson.
p. cm.
"This is a Borzoi book."
Includes index.
ISBN 978-0-307-59566-9
1. Cooking, Italian.   I. Manuali, Tanya Bastianich.   II. Title.
TX723.B31898 2012
641.5945—dc23   2012023455

Interior photographs by Marcus Nilsson
Jacket photograph by Marcus Nilsson
Jacket design by Kelly Blair
Designed by M. Kristen Bearse

Manufactured in the United States of America

First Edition

I would like to dedicate this book to all my loyal and committed fans. Through the years our friendship, bond, and trust have grown, and you have invited me into your homes and given me the opportunity to bring my Italian culture and flavors to your tables. You have shared my family and stories with your family and friends, have cooked many of my recipes, and have made some of them your favorites. I sense your appreciation for my recipes and my teachings through your e-mails and letters, and when we meet at special events, at book signings, and at my restaurants. I am immensely grateful to all of you—your hands and your kitchens bring Lidia's flavors alive. Thank you for allowing me to be part of your lives. I cherish and love being there.

Grazie,
Lidia

Contents

Sandwiches and Pizza

Primi—Pastas, Polentas, and Risottos

Desserts

Acknowledgments

I want to thank my great team for the creativity, enthusiasm, hard work, guidance, ideas, testing, and tasting that have gone into creating this book.

To Jessica Freeman Slade, thank you for your enthusiasm, for fresh perspectives, and for your incredibly thorough editing. And dear Ken Schneider, thank you for pulling it all so diligently together. Thank you also to the newest members of my Knopf team, Peter Gethers and Christina Malach. I look forward to working on many more projects together. Thanks to my ever-dependable kitchen companion, Amy Stevenson, for her shopping, testing, and contribution in writing to the recipes for the book as well as for being our culinary producer for the companion TV series.

For capturing my food through his eyes, I thank Marcus Nilsson. For tying up all the efforts and hard work into a wonderful design, thank you to Carol Devine Carson, Kelly Blair, and Kristen Bearse. A special thanks to my old friend Paul Bogaards for his endless efforts in marketing and promoting my works.

Thanks to Robert Barnett and Deneen Howell from Williams Connelly (wc.com) for helping me when I most needed assurance and security. This book would not have happened without your guidance and counsel.

A constant support throughout my life, Erminia, my mother, is a source of wisdom and good laughs for me. Thank you to my daughter, Tanya, for being my researching and writing companion as well as my confidant and partner, and thank you to my son, Joseph, a solid business partner; a family to be proud of. And not enough could be said about my love for my five little darlings: Olivia, Lorenzo, Miles, Ethan, and Julia. They make all the long hours and hard work easy; they make me so proud to be a grandmother.

I also want to thank my strong office team, led by Shelly Burgess Nicotra, who has stood by me for the past fifteen years: Lauren Falk, together with Sara Eagle from Knopf, who have kept me and my book in the limelight during and after my promotional travels; Rebecca Fornaby, who has kept our website visitors and Facebook fans informed; and Meghan Liu, my assistant, who has kept me and my ever-changing calendar updated and on schedule.

I would also like to thank those who make my show on public television possible. Thank you to the American Public Television team for always doing a stellar job distributing my show. And thanks to the wonderful team at my presenting station, WGBH in Boston. Their enthusiasm is contagious and their professionalism is exemplary. My show would not be possible without my sponsors: Grana Padano, Colavita, Perugina, and Cento.

While I am on the road filming and researching, there is an army of people who work and make sure my businesses continue on as I would have them. For their dedication and hard work, thank you to the staffs of Felidia, Becco, Del Posto, Lidia's Kansas City, Lidia's Pittsburgh, and Eataly.

And a big thank you to all my viewers and readers. I am so pleased you enjoy and am ever so grateful for your appreciation of the work I do.

Mille grazie!

Lidia

Introduction

I have written seven cookbooks thus far, and I'm so happy to have earned a place in your cookbook library. I'm sure that, as you read and cooked your way through each book, you found recipes that became your favorites. Some might be reliable recipes that are easy to cook, and others are probably more difficult recipes that are worth the effort, but my hope is that all of them are dishes that your family loves and that became part of your own traditions. As readers tell me about their experiences around the table, it's become clear that if I collected those favorite recipes and compiled them all accessibly in one book, it might be just the Lidia cookbook you are looking for. And here it is, just for you: *Lidia's Favorite Recipes*.

These recipes include not only your favorites, but mine as well, like My Mother's Chicken and Potatoes. It is a recipe that has remained a family favorite for the last four generations and I'm sure it had its family roots well before that. It has been slightly altered through the generations, but the deliciousness of this comfort food remains. There are also recipes that represent the flavors and story of my childhood, such as Polenta, and Swiss Chard Potatoes. There are recipes from some of my unforgettable trips, which will have you traveling through the regions of Italy—making Scaloppine Saltimbocca will transport you straight to Rome; Ziti with Broccoli Rabe and Sausages will take you to Puglia, in the heel of Italy; and Risotto con Porcini and Veal Ossobuco will make you feel like you're in Milan. Then there are recipes that speak of the Italian American story, which can be found in the flavors of my Spaghetti and Meatballs, Chicken Parmigiana, Baked Clams, Zucchini Roll-Ups, and many more. And as I put this book together, I added some of my new favorites, which I know you will try and love.

Family is very important to me, and I love to cook for my family and friends, so I included the simple and flavorful Italian dishes that you will love to prepare for *your* family and friends, like Minestrone, Meatloaf with Ricotta, and Sausage and Peppers. These recipes all make family-size quantities, and can also be divided and stored in the freezer for unexpected company, last-minute family visits, or even "I have no time to cook" nights. What's important is that these are all easy and delicious, and the warm, familiar flavors will bring your family

straight to the table. Today more than ever we want and need to gather around the table with our family and friends to escape our daily distractions, and what better way than with food that is luscious, nutritious, and cooked with love.

For most of these recipes, the ingredients are affordable and easy to find. This is especially true if you cook by the seasons—and, after all, that is the best way to cook. Today all of us care about eating consciously, sustainably, and responsibly, to keep our environment safe for future generations. Cooking and eating seasonal and local food, and not wasting a bit of it, is something all of us can do to make a difference while enjoying meals we love. A favorite dish is timeless, no matter your budget or the season, and I think you'll find that these favorite dishes of mine will remain your favorites as well.

Continue cooking, and *tutti a tavola a mangiare,*
Lidia Bastianich

APPETIZERS

SHRIMP AND MIXED BEAN SALAD

Insalata di Gamberi e Fagioli Misti

This is a favorite of mine, and I am sure it will become one for your family as well. I serve this dish at all of my family gatherings, especially when I am putting out a spread of salads, cheese, and sliced prosciutto. It is great when made with fresh cranberry and fava beans in spring, but it is equally good made with cooked dried cannellini beans or, for that matter, with other legumes, like *ceci* (chickpeas) and lentils. Both options are given here, so you can make it anytime.

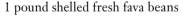

SERVES 6 OR MORE

1 pound shelled fresh fava beans

1 pound shelled fresh cranberry beans

½ small onion, cut in half

2 fresh or dried bay leaves

1 small carrot, sliced

1 stalk celery, cubed

1 pound large shrimp (about 20 to 30), shelled except for fantails, and deveined

3 tablespoons extra-virgin olive oil

3 tablespoons red wine vinegar

¼ teaspoon salt

Freshly ground black pepper to taste

1 pound dried Tuscan cannellini beans or other small white beans (such as baby lima or Great Northern), picked over and rinsed

2 fresh or dried bay leaves

1 teaspoon salt

If using dried cannellini beans instead of fresh cranberry beans: Place the dried beans in a medium-size bowl, and pour in enough cool water to cover by 4 inches. Soak the beans in a cool place for at least 8 hours. Drain the beans, and place them in a saucepan. Pour in enough cold water to cover them generously, and add the bay leaves. Bring the water to a boil over high heat. Keeping the pot at a simmer, cook the beans until tender, 40 to 60 minutes. Season the beans with salt about 10 minutes before the end of cooking. Drain the beans, remove the bay leaves, and let the beans cool.

If using fresh beans: Fill two separate pans with boiling water. Pour in the fresh beans, and cook until tender, about 4 and 8 minutes for the favas and cranberry beans respectively. Drain and refresh the beans under cold running water, and remove the outer skins from the favas.

Boil the onion, bay leaves, carrot, celery, and 6 cups water in a medium saucepan for 20 minutes. Add the shrimp, and cook until they have just turned opaque, about 1 minute. Drain the shrimp, and allow them to cool.

Whisk together the olive oil, vinegar, and salt and pepper in a serving bowl. Add the beans and shrimp, and toss to coat the ingredients completely, and serve.

SHRIMP "ALLA BUONAVIA"

Scampi alla Buonavia

I have been making this dish for forty years, since Buonavia, my first restaurant, opened in 1971, and it's become one of my favorites after so long. In this dish, high heat and speed are essential. Make sure that the pan is good and hot when you add the shrimp, and that it is wide enough to hold all the shrimp pieces in a single layer (so the pan doesn't cool down as the shrimp go in). Be sure to have all your ingredients right by the stove—once the shrimp go into the pan, it's full speed ahead!

SERVES 6

3 tablespoons extra-virgin olive oil, plus more for finishing dish

3 cloves garlic, finely chopped

1 pound (about 25) extra-large shrimp, completely shelled, deveined, and cut into 3 pieces

1 tablespoon chopped fresh chives

½ cup dry white wine

4 tablespoons unsalted butter, cut into 4 pieces

1 tablespoon freshly squeezed lemon juice

1 tablespoon chopped fresh Italian parsley, plus parsley sprigs for garnish if desired

½ teaspoon hot red pepper flakes

Salt to taste

6 slices Italian bread (about ¼ inch thick and 2½ inches wide), toasted and kept warm

1 lemon, cut into slices

Heat the olive oil in a large skillet over medium heat. Add the garlic, and cook, shaking the pan, until light golden, about 2 minutes. Raise the heat to high, add the shrimp, and cook until they turn bright pink and are seared on all sides, about 2 minutes. Stir in the chopped chives, then add the wine, butter, and lemon juice. Bring to a boil, and cook until the shrimp are barely opaque in the center and the sauce is reduced by half, about 2 minutes. Stir in the chopped parsley and crushed red pepper. Season with salt.

Place a piece of warm toast in the center of each of six warm plates. Spoon the shrimp and sauce over the toast, drizzling some of the sauce around the toast. Decorate the plates with lemon slices, and with the parsley sprigs if desired.

OCTOPUS AND POTATO SALAD

Insalata di Polipo e Patate

There was a time when Americans were squeamish about eating octopus, but now this is a favorite and a staple on the menu at Felidia. Octopus has come of age as a delicious ingredient, and any respectable restaurant has an appetizer that includes it; at my house, it has always been popular, even with the kids.

This salad can be made in advance, but just keep in mind that the potatoes get hard and waxy when refrigerated, so refrigerate the octopus but leave the potatoes at room temperature. You can toss them together just before serving. Your fishmonger (or supermarket fish counter) will often have tenderized octopus, which most likely has been defrosted. Usually an octopus weighs about 2 or 3 pounds, but shrinks to half its original size when cooked.

For this recipe I recommend Idaho potatoes, but it's nice to mix these up with whatever is in season, be it Red Bliss, fingerlings, or the purple Peruvian potatoes that are now all the rage.

SERVES 6

2-to-3-pound octopus, cleaned

1 wine cork

2 fresh bay leaves, or 3 dried

Salt and freshly ground black pepper to taste

2 medium Idaho potatoes, whole

5 tablespoons olive oil

3 tablespoons red wine vinegar

1 red onion, thinly sliced

2 tablespoons chopped fresh Italian parsley

Lemon wedges for garnish

Place the octopus, wine cork, bay leaves, and salt and pepper in a large pot. Cover generously with water, and bring to a boil. Reduce the heat, and cook the octopus at a vigorous simmer until tender but slightly *al dente*, about 25 minutes. (Test periodically by inserting the tines of a fork into the thickest part of the octopus. It is done when the fork penetrates easily and can be removed with only a little resistance.)

Meanwhile, cover the potatoes with cold water in a second pot, and bring to a boil. Cook about 25 minutes, until just tender, then cool, peel, and cut them into 1-inch cubes.

Drain the octopus, discarding the bay leaves and cork. Cut the tentacles away where they join the head. Clean the octopus head, which looks like a pouch the size of your fist, by squeezing out the core with your fingers, and cut the meat into thin slices. Cut the tentacles into inch-long pieces, and toss the octopus pieces with the warm potatoes. Toss with the olive oil, red-wine vinegar, onion, and parsley. Place on a plate, garnish with lemon wedges, and serve.

STUFFED VEGETABLES

Verdure Ripiene

Italians will stuff just about any vegetable with either bread or meat, and stuffed vegetables are a favorite along the Italian peninsula. A platter of baked stuffed vegetables is a delight that you see in many restaurants as you travel around Italy, but the array is never exactly the same, with vegetables varying from region to region. There are many ways to stuff an Italian vegetable, but this recipe is one of my favorites.

Here I give you this delicious and easy bread stuffing, along with procedures for preparing and baking a few of the most typical vegetables—bell peppers, mushrooms, sweet onions, tomatoes, and zucchini. I've kept the amount of the vegetables loose, so you can make as many as you want and change the vegetables according to season, creating a new recipe every time.

MAKES ABOUT 3 DOZEN VEGETABLE MORSELS

FOR THE STUFFING

4 cups 1-inch cubes of day-old or dry country bread, crusts removed (about 4 thick slices)

1 cup milk

¼ ounce dried porcini (about ¼ cup loosely packed pieces), soaked in 2 cups warm water

1 cup finely chopped scallions

10 large fresh basil leaves, finely chopped

½ cup freshly grated Grana Padano or Parmigiano-Reggiano cheese

1 teaspoon kosher salt

2 large eggs, lightly beaten

FOR THE VEGETABLE ASSORTMENT

2 or more medium zucchini (6 inches long)

2 or more red or other colorful bell peppers

12 or more large white stuffing mushrooms

3 or more small ripe tomatoes

2 or more large Vidalia or other sweet, flat onions

1½ teaspoons kosher salt

½ cup extra-virgin olive oil, plus more as needed

Butter for the baking dishes

½ cup freshly grated Grana Padano or Parmigiano-Reggiano cheese

To make the stuffing: Pour the milk over the bread cubes in a bowl; toss well, and let sit for a couple of minutes. When they're softened, gather and press the cubes together, squeezing out any excess milk, and return the moistened bread to a dry bowl, tearing it into shreds with your fingers.

Lift the rehydrated porcini pieces from the soaking liquid, squeeze firmly (saving all the liquid), and chop them into fine bits. Scatter the chopped porcini, scallions, basil, grated cheese, and 1 teaspoon salt on top of the torn bread, and toss to combine. Stir in the beaten eggs with a wooden spoon (or mix with your hands) to form a well-blended, fairly dense stuffing.

To prepare zucchini for stuffing: Trim off the ends, and slice the squashes in half lengthwise. Scoop out the central pulp and any seeds with a teaspoon or melon baller, so each half resembles a hollowed boat. Cut the long halves crosswise into serving-size pieces, about 3 inches long.

To prepare the bell peppers for stuffing: slice them lengthwise in half, starting at the stem, or in thirds if very large; trim away the stem and all seeds and fibers, forming cuplike pieces.

To prepare the mushrooms, tomatoes, and onions: Pull out the stems of the mushrooms, leaving the hollow caps for stuffing. Cut the tomatoes in half crosswise, and squeeze out the seeds to make concavities for stuffing. Peel the onions, and cut them crosswise into ¾-inch-thick slices.

When all the vegetables are prepped and all but onions are hollowed, put the pieces (except the onion slices) in a large bowl. Season with salt. Brush some of the oil on the onion slices, keeping them whole. Then toss the remaining olive oil and ½ teaspoon salt with the vegetables in the bowl.

To stuff and bake the vegetables: Butter the baking dishes, arrange a rack (or two, if necessary) in the oven, and heat to 425 degrees F. For the zucchini, peppers, tomatoes, and mushrooms, fill the cavities with about a tablespoon of stuffing and arrange all the pieces in a baking dish, with a bit of space between them. Lay the onion slices flat in the dish, and mound a spoonful of stuffing on top of each slice.

When the dishes are filled (but not crowded), sprinkle all the vegetable pieces evenly with the grated cheese and remaining ½ teaspoon salt. Scrape any olive oil left in the vegetable bowl over the stuffed pieces, and pour the reserved porcini-soaking liquid (leaving behind any gritty residue) into the bottom of each baking dish. Cover each dish with a tent of foil, pressing it against the dish sides; make sure the foil doesn't touch the stuffing or tops of the vegetables.

Bake 30 minutes, until the vegetables have started to soften and release juices, then remove the foil tents and bake until the stuffing is crispy and brown, another 30 minutes or so. Switch the position of the dishes in the oven once or twice, so all the pieces cook and color evenly. Serve hot from the oven, or let the vegetables cool and serve at room temperature.

EGG-BATTERED ZUCCHINI ROLL-UPS

Involtini di Zucchini Fritti

This is a picnic favorite: the bite-size rolls are perfect to pop into your mouth at room temperature. Zucchini is readily available and affordable, especially in the summertime, and when prepared with a little imagination, as in this dish, it is delicious and festive-looking. This favorite recipe first appeared in *Lidia's Family Table*. I have literally grown up on zucchini prepared this way—sliced into thin strips, dipped in egg, and fried. It was one of my favorite vegetables when I was little, and my mother often made our school lunch sandwiches with these strips.

SERVES 10 AS HORS D'OEUVRES OR 6 AS A SIDE DISH

2 pounds (5 or 6) small zucchini

2 cups all-purpose flour for dredging

5 large eggs

¾ teaspoon salt, or more to taste

Freshly ground black pepper to taste

Canola oil for frying (2 cups or more, depending on skillet size)

1 or 2 tablespoons well-drained tiny brined capers

Freshly squeezed juice of about ½ lemon

To coat and fry the zucchini: Rinse and dry the zucchini, and trim off the stem and blossom ends. Use a sharp knife to slice the squash lengthwise into strips about ⅛ inch thick, flexible but not paper-thin. (You should get five or six strips from each small zucchini.)

Dump the flour into a wide bowl or shallow dish. Beat the eggs well in another wide bowl, stirring in ½ teaspoon of the salt and some grinds of pepper. Set a wide colander on a plate, to drain the battered strips before frying. Tumble five or six zucchini strips at a time in the flour, coating them well on both sides. Shake off the loose flour, and slide the strips into the beaten eggs. Turn and separate the strips with a fork so they're covered with batter; pick them up one at a time, letting the excess egg drip back into the bowl; lay the strips in the colander. Dredge and batter all the zucchini strips this way, and let them drain. Add the egg drippings collected under the colander to the batter, if you need more.

Pour ⅓ inch of canola oil into a deep skillet, and set it over medium-high heat. Cover a baking sheet or large platter with several layers of paper toweling, and place it near the stove. When the oil is very hot but not smoking, test it by dropping in half a strip of battered zucchini. It should sizzle actively and begin to crisp around the edges, but not smoke or darken. When the oil is ready, quickly slip several strips into the skillet, using kitchen tongs or a long fork to avoid spatters of hot oil. Don't crowd the strips—no more than seven at a time in a 12-inch pan—so they crisp quickly and won't absorb oil. Fry the zucchini strips

(recipe continues)

in batches, and when they are golden on both sides, remove them and set them on the paper towels to drain. Salt them lightly, and lay additional paper towels over the fried strips, so you can layer over them the next ones to come out of the skillet. Let the slices cool for a few minutes.

To form the roll-ups: Place a fried strip on your work table, with the wider end (from the blossom end of the zucchini) closer to you. Place three or four capers on that end, then roll the strip tightly, enclosing the capers in the center. Weave a toothpick all the way through the roll-up, so it stays together. Roll up all the strips, or as many as you want.

Just before serving, stand the roll-ups on end and squeeze drops of lemon juice all over the spiral tops. Arrange them on a serving platter. (If you like capers as much as I do, scatter another teaspoon or so of drained capers all over.)

FRIED MOZZARELLA SKEWERS

Spiedini alla Romana

No one can resist fried cheese, and these Italian mini-sandwiches are no exception. They are a classic dish in Italian American cooking, and especially beloved by anyone fond of grilled cheese sandwiches. Firm white bread is recommended in the recipe, but multigrain or whole-wheat will be just as delicious.

SERVES 4

2 tablespoons extra-virgin olive oil

5 cloves garlic, chopped

4 anchovy fillets

3 tablespoons drained tiny capers in brine

2 tablespoons unsalted butter

½ cup dry white wine

3 tablespoons freshly squeezed lemon juice

8 slices firm white bread, crusts removed

12 ounces fresh mozzarella, thinly sliced

All-purpose flour for dredging

2 large eggs

2 tablespoons milk

Vegetable oil for frying

1 tablespoon chopped fresh Italian parsley

Make the sauce: Pour the olive oil into a large skillet, and set over medium-high heat. When the oil is hot, add the chopped garlic, and cook until it is sizzling and fragrant, taking care not to burn it. Add the anchovies and capers, and stir until they both dissolve into the oil. Plop in the butter; once it is melted, pour in the white wine and lemon juice. Bring to an energetic simmer, and cook until reduced by half, about 6 to 7 minutes. Remove and keep warm.

Lay four slices of bread on your work surface. Top with the sliced mozzarella, trimming the cheese to fit within the edges of the bread. Top with remaining bread to make four sandwiches, and seal each sandwich at each corner with a toothpick.

Spread the flour on a rimmed plate. Beat the eggs and milk together in a wide, shallow bowl. Heat about ½ inch vegetable oil in a skillet over medium heat; the oil is ready when a crust of bread sizzles on contact.

Dredge the sandwiches well in the flour, making sure to coat all sides and tap off the excess. Soak the sandwiches on all sides in the egg, letting the excess egg drip back into the bowl. Carefully ease the sandwiches into the oil, and fry until they're golden brown on both sides and the cheese is melted, about 1 to 2 minutes per side. Remove the sandwiches, and drain well on paper towels. Remove the toothpicks from sandwiches, and use a serrated knife to cut them in half on the diagonal.

Return the sauce to a simmer, and stir in the parsley. Spread the sauce on four serving plates, then top each plate with a sandwich and serve hot.

BREAD AND TOMATO SALAD
Panzanella

Panzanella has become a favorite dish to cook back home among people who have traveled to Italy, evoking memories of Tuscan sunshine and a good glass of Chianti. It's so easy to make that anyone who has been to Italy brings this recipe back. The version I share with you here is made with onions—red onions, or even sweet onions like Vidalia, will be delicious. You can serve this salad on its own, or with a plate of mozzarella and prosciutto, as a great starter or as a main course.

Country bread is recommended, but rustic whole-grain or whole-wheat is a great substitute.

SERVES 6

1 pound 2-day-old country-style bread, crusts removed, cut into ½-inch cubes (about 8 cups)

2 pounds ripe tomatoes at room temperature, cored, seeded, and cut into ½-inch cubes (about 4 cups)

1 cup coarsely diced red onion

12 fresh basil leaves, shredded, plus a few extra sprigs for garnish

5 tablespoons extra-virgin olive oil

3 tablespoons red-wine vinegar

Salt and freshly ground black pepper to taste

Toss the bread, tomatoes, onion, and shredded basil leaves in a large bowl until well mixed. Drizzle the olive oil and vinegar over the salad, and toss to mix thoroughly. Season to taste with salt and pepper, and let stand 10 minutes before serving. Decorate with sprigs of fresh basil.

LOBSTER SALAD WITH FRESH TOMATOES

Aragosta alla Catalana

There is nothing I enjoy more than working my way through a lobster or crab, plucking the meat out of the shell and savoring each morsel. The succulent flavors of the salad and the fun of picking at the lobster are the draw of this dish, but I also love the beautiful colors of the salad.

If you do not feel like working through lobster shells, shrimp will work as well, as long as you are sure not to overcook it.

SERVES 6 AS AN APPETIZER SALAD,
OR 4 AS A MAIN-COURSE SALAD

1 teaspoon kosher salt, plus 6 tablespoons for the lobster pot

Two 1¼-pound live lobsters

3 or 4 ripe fresh tomatoes (about 1½ pounds), or 1 pound sweet, ripe cherry tomatoes

2 or 3 tender stalks celery with a nice amount of leaves

Freshly squeezed juice of 2 large lemons (about ⅓ cup)

2 large hard-cooked eggs, peeled and chopped

¼ teaspoon hot red pepper flakes, or to taste

¾ cup extra-virgin olive oil

2 tablespoons chopped fresh Italian parsley

Fill a large pot with 6 quarts water, add 6 tablespoons salt, and bring to a rolling boil. When the water is at a rolling boil, drop in the lobsters, and cook them, uncovered, for exactly 10 minutes after the water returns to the boiling point (and then keep it boiling). At the end of 10 minutes (or a couple of minutes

longer if the lobsters are larger than 1¼ pounds), lift the lobsters from the pot, rinse with cold water, drain, and let them cool.

Core and cut the tomatoes into wedges, about 1 inch thick (if you have cherry tomatoes, cut them in half). Chop the celery stalks crosswise into 1-inch pieces, and roughly chop the leaves. Toss the tomatoes and celery together in a large bowl with ½ teaspoon of the salt.

When the lobsters are cool enough to handle, twist and pull off the claws and knuckle segments where the knuckles attach to the front of the body. Lay the clawless lobsters flat on a cutting board, and split them in half lengthwise, from head to tail, with a heavy chef's knife. Separate the meaty tail pieces from the carcass (or body) of the four split halves.

Cut the lobster body meat and shell into pieces of whatever size you like, putting the pieces in a large mixing bowl as you work. Separate the knuckles from the claws, and crack open the shells of both knuckles and hard claw pincers with the thick edge of the knife blade, or kitchen shears, exposing the meat. Chop the knuckles into pieces at the joints.

Cut the tail pieces crosswise into chunks, or leave them whole (which I prefer). Cut the carcass pieces crosswise in two, with the walking legs still attached (though you can cut them off). I like to leave the tomalley and roe in the body pieces, as a special treat while eating the salad. (As an alternative, remove the tomalley and roe and whisk them into the dressing. Or you can remove them and discard, if they're not to your liking.)

To make the dressing: Whisk together the lemon juice, chopped eggs, hot red pepper flakes, and remaining ½ teaspoon salt. Pour in the olive oil in a slow stream, whisking steadily to incorporate it into a smooth dressing.

To serve: Add the tomatoes and celery to the bowl of lobster pieces. Pour in the dressing, and tumble everything together until evenly coated. Scatter the parsley on top. Arrange the salad on a large platter, or compose individual servings on salad plates.

RICE AND ZUCCHINI CROSTATA

Torta di Riso e Zucchine

The dough for this crostata, or savory tart, is easy to roll out, and the filling is inexpensive and easy to make as well. At my house we make it whenever we expect guests, or just the family, to come over, and we never have leftovers. People just keep walking by the plate, picking up a piece or two, and popping it into their mouths. This is my daughter Tanya's favorite when she is expecting guests, because it can be made in advance and kept warm in the oven, ready for passing as an hors d'oeuvre with a glass of Prosecco.

There's one important step to note here: since squash is a watery vegetable, and rice is dry and starchy, they need to steep together. Steeping allows the rice to extract most of the vegetal water from the zucchini, softening the grain enough to cook during the baking time, and the result is a moist, creamy, and flavorful filling.

For the change of seasons, the zucchini in this recipe can be easily replaced with winter squash, making it a festive fall-winter recipe.

MAKES 15 OR MORE APPETIZER SLICES, OR SEVERAL DOZEN HORS D'OEUVRES

FOR THE DOUGH

2 cups all-purpose flour, plus more for rolling out the dough

1 teaspoon kosher salt

½ cup extra-virgin olive oil

⅓ cup cold water, plus more as needed

FOR THE FILLING

1 pound small zucchini

½ cup Italian short-grain rice (such as Arborio, Carnaroli, or Vialone Nano)

2 cups ricotta, drained overnight

1 cup grated Grana Padano or Parmigiano-Reggiano cheese

2 bunches scallions, finely chopped (about 2 cups)

3 large eggs, lightly beaten

2 cups milk

2 teaspoons kosher salt

Butter for the baking pan

To make the dough: Pour the flour and salt into a food processor fitted with the metal blade. Pulse a few seconds to aerate the dough. Mix the oil and water together and, with the processor running, pour the liquid through the feed tube and mix for about 30 seconds, until a soft dough forms and gathers on the blade. If it doesn't form, the dough is probably too dry, so add more water in small amounts until you have a smooth, very soft dough.

(recipe continues)

Turn the dough out onto a lightly floured surface, and knead by hand for a minute. Pat into a rectangle, and wrap loosely in plastic wrap. Let rest at room temperature for ½ hour.

To make the filling: Shred the zucchini on the coarse holes of a box grater into a large bowl. Toss the rice and shredded zucchini together, and let sit for 30 minutes to an hour, until the grains have absorbed the vegetable liquid. Fold in the ricotta (breaking up any lumps), then the grated cheese, scallions, beaten eggs, milk, and salt, stirring thoroughly until mixed.

Preheat the oven to 375 degrees F. Spread the butter on the bottom and sides of a 12-by-18-inch rimmed baking sheet (a half-sheet pan).

Roll the dough on a lightly floured surface to a rectangle that's at least 4 inches longer and wider than the baking sheet. Transfer the dough to the pan, either by folding it in quarters and lifting it onto the sheet, or by rolling it up around a floured rolling pin and then unfurling it over the baking sheet. When the dough is centered over the pan, gently press its center flat against the bottom and rim of the pan, leaving even flaps of overhanging dough on all sides. (If the dough tears as you are moving it, patch it with a bit of dough from the edges.)

Scrape the filling into the dough-lined pan, and spread it to fill the crust in an even layer. Fold the dough flaps over the top of the filling, pleating the corners, to form a top crust border that looks like a picture frame, with the filling exposed in the middle.

Set the pan in the oven, and bake until the crust is deep golden brown and the filling is set, about 50 minutes. About halfway through the baking time, turn the pan in the oven, back to front, for even color and cooking.

Cool the torta on a wire rack for at least 30 minutes to set the filling before slicing. The torta can be served warm or at room temperature, cut into pieces in any shape you like—squares, rectangles, triangles, or diamonds.

GARLIC BREAD

Pane Strofinato all'Aglio

Everybody loves warm bread when it arrives at the table, and when it has the scent of garlic wafting from it, you know it has the Italian touch. The goal in making a good garlic bread is to rub the bread with the crushed garlic clove, not to load it with chopped garlic; remember, just the essence is enough to gratify your senses.

SERVES 4

3 tablespoons extra-virgin olive oil

3 cloves garlic, crushed and peeled

12-inch loaf Italian bread without seeds

1 teaspoon dried oregano

Kosher salt for seasoning

Combine the olive oil and garlic in a small bowl, and steep about 30 minutes, to let the flavors mingle.

Preheat the oven to 400 degrees F. Split the bread in half lengthwise, then cut in half crosswise, to make four pieces. Set the pieces, cut side up, on a baking sheet, and brush the bread with the flavored oil, rubbing with the garlic cloves and leaving them on top. Sprinkle with the dried oregano.

Bake until the bread is golden and crispy, about 4 to 5 minutes. Remove any large garlic pieces, and lightly season the bread with salt before serving.

VARIATION: Garlic Bread Topped with Cheese (Pane Strofinato con Formaggio): Substitute ¼ cup grated Grana Padano or Parmigiano-Reggiano for the oregano.

VARIATION: Garlic Bread Rubbed with Tomatoes (Pane Strofinato con Pomodoro): Cut some ripe tomatoes in half crosswise. While the baked bread is still hot, rub cut surfaces of the bread with the tomato halves, until the bread has absorbed the tomato juices, and the tomato pulp has rubbed onto the bread. Season lightly with salt, drizzle some extra-virgin olive oil on top, and serve immediately.

BAKED CLAMS OREGANATA

Vongole Ripiene al Forno

The briny flavor of the clams with the crispy breadcrumb coating makes this dish one of my favorite appetizers, and it is also a go-to recipe in *Lidia's Italy in America.* The topping used here for the clams is also great to put on top of fish such as halibut, salmon, or sole when baking. Clams Oreganata have become a classic Italian American dish, much beloved and often found on mixed-antipasto plates.

SERVES 6

36 littleneck clams, shucked, half the shells reserved, juices reserved and strained

1½ cups fine dry breadcrumbs

½ cup finely chopped red bell pepper

¼ cup finely chopped fresh Italian parsley

1 teaspoon dried oregano

½ teaspoon kosher salt

6 tablespoons extra-virgin olive oil

½ cup dry white wine

Lemon wedges for serving (optional)

Preheat the oven to 425 degrees F.

Coarsely chop the shucked clams, and put in a large bowl. Add the breadcrumbs, bell pepper, parsley, oregano, and salt. Drizzle with 2 tablespoons olive oil, and toss with a fork to combine.

Stuff the clam shells with the filling, and place on a rimmed baking sheet. Drizzle each clam with a little of the reserved clam juice, pouring any extra juice, along with the white wine, into the bottom of the pan. Drizzle the clams with 3 tablespoons olive oil, and drizzle the remaining tablespoon oil in the bottom of the pan.

Bake until the clam stuffing is browned and crispy, about 15 minutes. To serve, set the clams on a plate with the remaining sauce and a wedge of fresh lemon if desired.

RICE BALLS

Arancini di Riso

These are another favorite appetizer in Italy, the United States, and my house for sure. Kids love them, particularly when the hidden treasure at the center is savory prosciutto and oozing cheese. Pop these in your mouth, making sure, of course, they are not too hot. Arborio rice is recommended in the recipe, but this dish can be made with brown rice as well; just make sure you cook it long enough, and you will need to use a bit more stock.

MAKES ABOUT 2 DOZEN

3 tablespoons extra-virgin olive oil

1 medium onion, finely chopped

1 cup finely diced ham or prosciutto (about 3 ounces)

2 cups Arborio rice

1 cup dry white wine

5 cups chicken stock

½ teaspoon kosher salt, plus more for seasoning

1 cup frozen peas, thawed

1 cup grated Grana Padano or Parmigiano-Reggiano cheese

10 fresh basil leaves, chopped

4 ounces fresh mozzarella, cut into ½-inch cubes (you'll need about 24 cubes)

1 cup all-purpose flour

2 cups fine dry breadcrumbs

2 large eggs

Vegetable oil for frying

Heat the olive oil in a medium saucepan; when the oil is hot, add the onion and cook until softened, about 3 to 4 minutes. Add the ham or prosciutto, and cook a few minutes, until the meat begins to render its fat.

Add the rice, and cook to coat the rice in the oil and fat. Pour in the wine, bring to a simmer, and cook until the wine is almost reduced away. Add 3 cups hot chicken stock and the salt; cover, and simmer until the chicken stock is absorbed by the rice, about 7 to 8 minutes. Add the remaining 2 cups stock, and cover, letting the rice cook until *al dente*, about 6 to 7 minutes more. Stir in peas toward the end, and mix well; spread the rice on a rimmed sheet pan to cool.

When the rice is cool, put it in a bowl and stir in the grated cheese and chopped basil. Scoop out about ⅓ cup rice, roll into a loose ball, then poke a cube of mozzarella into the center. Pat firmly to form a tight ball around the cheese.

Spread the flour and breadcrumbs on two rimmed plates, and beat the eggs in a shallow bowl. Dredge the arancini in the flour, shaking off the excess. Dip them one by one in the beaten egg, letting the excess drip back into the bowl. Roll in the breadcrumbs to coat thoroughly.

Pour an inch of vegetable oil into a large straight-sided skillet set over medium heat. Fry in batches, taking care not to crowd the skillet, turning on all sides, until golden, about 3 minutes per batch. Drain the arancini on paper towels, and season with salt while still warm.

SALADS AND SOUPS

SCALLION AND ASPARAGUS SALAD

Insalata di Scalogno e Asparagi

Hands down, this is one of my favorite dishes, in part because of who first served it to me. My grandmother would often make this lovely spring salad, occasionally tossing in a boiled egg or two. This salad is delicious as an antipasto or a first course, or as a side dish to grilled meat and fish.

SERVES 6

1½ pounds fresh asparagus

¾ pound scallions

1 teaspoon salt

3½ tablespoons extra-virgin olive oil

1½ tablespoons red wine vinegar

Freshly ground black pepper to taste

3 hard-cooked eggs, peeled

Using a vegetable peeler, shave off the skin from the bottom 3 inches or so of each asparagus stalk, so they cook evenly. Snap off the hard stubs at the bottom—they'll break naturally at the right point as you bend the bottom of the asparagus. To prepare the scallions, trim the roots and the wilted ends of the green leaves. Peel off the loose layers at the white end, so the scallions are all tight, trim, and about 6 inches long.

Bring 1 quart of water (or enough to cover the vegetables) to a boil in a wide, deep skillet, and add the asparagus and scallions. Adjust the heat to maintain a bubbling boil, and poach the vegetables, uncovered, for about 6 minutes or more, until they are tender but not falling apart, cooked through but not mushy. To check doneness, pick up an asparagus spear by its middle with tongs: it should be a little droopy, but not collapsing.

As soon as they are done, lift out the vegetables with tongs and lay them in a colander (any fat asparagus spears may take a little longer, so leave them in a few minutes more). Hold the colander under cold running water to stop the cooking. Drain briefly, then spread on kitchen towels and pat dry; sprinkle about ½ teaspoon salt over them.

Slice the asparagus and the scallions into 1-inch lengths, and pile them loosely in a mixing bowl. Drizzle the oil and vinegar over the top, and sprinkle on the remaining salt and several grinds of black pepper. Toss well, but don't break up the vegetables. Quarter the eggs into wedges, and slice each wedge into two or three pieces; scatter these in the bowl, and fold in with the vegetables. Taste, and adjust the dressing. Chill the salad briefly, then arrange it on a serving platter or on salad plates.

CELERY AND ARTICHOKE SALAD

Insalata di Sedano e Carciofi

Celery is not used often enough as a principal salad ingredient, but the inner stalks of the head have a wonderful freshness, flavor, and delicacy when thinly sliced. (Make sure to include the tender inside leaves of the celery as well.) My readers rave about this recipe, and love the crunchy texture and the savory shaved cheese.

SERVES 6

2 whole lemons

1 quart cold water

6 firm small artichokes, no wider than 3 inches

8 to 12 tender stalks celery with leaves, from the inner part of the head

FOR THE DRESSING

1½ tablespoons freshly squeezed lemon juice, or more to taste

6 tablespoons extra-virgin olive oil

¾ teaspoon salt, or more to taste

¼-pound chunk of Grana Padano or Parmigiano-Reggiano cheese, or more to taste

Cut the 2 lemons in half, and squeeze their juice into a bowl with a quart of cold water. The acidulated water will keep the artichoke slices from discoloring after you cut them.

To trim the artichokes: Work with one artichoke at a time. Trim off the thick outside leaves until you reach the tender, pale inside leaves. Cut off the tough bottom of the stem but leave most of it (an inch or so) attached to the globe. With a vegetable peeler or paring knife, peel off the outer skin of the short stem, exposing the fresh layer underneath. Next, at about a third of the way down, cut straight across the pointed top of the artichoke, removing the tips of the leaves. Drop the trimmed artichoke into the acidulated water, and trim the rest of them in this way, submerging them all in the bowl.

To prepare the celery: Trim off the tender leaves, and slice each stalk on the diagonal into ⅛-inch-thick delicate, translucent crescents. Gently cut the tender leaves to pieces of about ¾ inch, then toss all the celery—about 2 cups—into a large mixing bowl.

To make and dress the salad: When you're ready to serve the salad, remove a trimmed artichoke from the lemon water, and cut, from stem to top, into thin ⅛-inch slices; add the slices to the bowl with the celery. Quickly slice all the artichokes this way, then toss the celery and artichoke slices together with the 1½ tablespoons lemon juice, the olive oil, and the salt.

Shave about twenty-four large, delicate flakes of Grana Padano or Parmigiano-Reggiano from the chunk of cheese, using a vegetable peeler or a sharp knife: each shaving should be a couple of inches long and an inch or two wide. Gently fold the shavings of cheese into the sliced vegetables. Taste, and adjust dressing. Arrange the salad on a serving platter, or portion it on salad plates. Shave more flakes of cheese, and scatter a dozen or more over the platter, or place three or four flakes on top of each individual serving.

ROASTED BEET AND BEET GREENS SALAD WITH APPLES AND GOAT CHEESE

Insalata di Barbabietole con Mele e Formaggio Caprino

A beet salad with goat cheese has become ubiquitous on restaurant menus, a favorite throughout America. This version is a bit different, using the beet greens as well—most people think of only the beet bulb itself, but the greens are as delicious and nutritious as the root, and this is a great way to use them in a salad. It is best with small, firm beets with fresh, unblemished greens, a crisp, tart apple, and crumbly goat cheese. Roasting the beets to intensify the sweetness yields the best results.

SERVES 6

10 to 12 small yellow and red beets with greens attached (about 3 pounds total)

½ teaspoon salt

⅓ cup extra-virgin olive oil

⅓ cup good-quality balsamic vinegar

Freshly ground black pepper to taste

1 medium tart, crisp apple (such as Granny Smith)

4 ounces or so slightly aged goat cheese

Preheat the oven to 400 degrees F.

Slice the greens off, leaving a tiny bit of stem on the top of the beets, then scrub the beets and poke each of them with a fork a few times. Put them all in a shallow baking dish, uncovered, with a ⅛ inch of water covering the bottom. Roast the beets—the water will actually steam them a bit first—until they are shriveled, dark, and caramelized outside, and tender all the way through (when poked with a knife)—45 minutes to 1½ hours, depending on size. Let them cool completely.

Rinse the beet greens well, trimming off the tough parts of the stems, and cut the softer stem pieces from the leaves. Bring a big pan of water to the boil, then drop in the stems and cook for about 10 minutes; then add the greens. Cook for 20 minutes more, or until the stems are quite soft. Drain in a sieve; sprinkle ¼ teaspoon salt over the hot greens, and let them cool. Peel the cooled beets, removing all the skin, the stem base, and the root tip, exposing the gleaming flesh. Cut in wedges, and place in a big mixing bowl. Cut the greens (both leaves and stems) into 2-inch lengths, and toss with the beet wedges.

Whisk together the oil and vinegar, with the remaining ¼ teaspoon salt and some grinds of pepper. Drizzle the dressing over the beets, and toss to combine. Core and slice the apple into thin matchsticks. Arrange the dressed beets on a serving platter or portion them on salad plates; fold in the apple pieces, then crumble goat cheese on top just before serving.

RED CABBAGE AND BACON SALAD

Insalata di Cavolo Rosso e Pancetta

This salad is one of my favorites because of the crunchiness in every bite. Be certain to slice the cabbage very thinly, using either a mandoline slicer or a food processor. It is a great winter salad, and delicious with the crisp bacon, but I sometimes enjoy it with just the olive-oil-and-balsamic-vinegar dressing.

SERVES 4 TO 6

1 small head red cabbage, very finely shredded

¼ cup extra-virgin olive oil

1 pound sliced bacon, cut into 1-inch pieces

5 tablespoons balsamic vinegar

Kosher salt

Shred the red cabbage into a large serving bowl. Heat 1 tablespoon olive oil in a large skillet over medium heat. Cook the bacon until crisp, about 5 to 6 minutes, then remove to a paper-towel-lined plate. Pour off most of the fat, and return the pan to the heat.

Add the remaining olive oil and the vinegar to the skillet. Bring the liquid to an energetic simmer, and pour the hot sauce over the cabbage in the bowl. Mop out the skillet with a handful of the cabbage to get the crusty bits from the bottom of the pan, and add to the bowl. Season with the salt, and toss well so the cabbage doesn't stick together. Serve warm or at room temperature.

RICE AND POTATO SOUP

Minestra di Riso e Patate

This is the soup my grandmother made most often, and definitely one of my favorites. It is one of the simplest soups to make, and I am sure it will become a favorite of your family, too.

To make this soup, be sure you save the rinds of Grana Padano or Parmigiano-Reggiano when you have finished grating it. Keep the rinds in the freezer, wrapped in plastic, until you are ready to toss them into soups; they add much flavor and complexity to any soup.

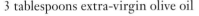

MAKES ABOUT 2 QUARTS, SERVING 8

3 tablespoons extra-virgin olive oil

2 large baking (Idaho) potatoes, peeled and cut into ⅓-inch cubes

2 medium carrots, trimmed, peeled, and coarsely shredded

2 center stalks celery, trimmed and diced

Salt

2 teaspoons tomato paste

10 cups hot water

2 fresh or dried bay leaves

Leftover rind of the grated Grana Padano or Parmigiano-Reggiano cheese, washed

Freshly ground black pepper

1 cup long-grain rice

½ cup chopped fresh Italian parsley leaves

¼ cup freshly grated Grana Padano or Parmigiano-Reggiano cheese

In a deep, heavy 4-to-5-quart pot, heat the olive oil over medium heat. Add the potatoes, and cook, stirring occasionally, until lightly browned, about 5 minutes. (It's fine if the potatoes stick; just adjust the level of heat to prevent the bits of potato that stick from getting too dark.) Stir in the carrots and celery, and cook, stirring with a wooden spoon, until the carrots are softened, 2 to 3 minutes. Season lightly with salt, then stir in the tomato paste to coat the vegetables. Pour in the hot water and bay leaves, then bring to a boil, scraping up the bits of stuck potato. Add the washed cheese rinds, adjust the level of heat to keep soup at a simmer, and season the soup lightly with salt and pepper. Cover the pot, and simmer until the potatoes begin to fall apart, about 40 minutes.

Stir the rice into the hot soup and let simmer, stirring well, until the rice is tender but still firm, about 12 minutes. Remove the bay leaves. Sprinkle the parsley into the soup, and season with grated cheese and salt and pepper to taste.

TOMATO AND BREAD SOUP

Pappa al Pomodoro

This soup will bring Tuscany to your table, and it is delicious warm, or served at room temperature on a hot summer day. It is a great soup to make in the summer, when the tomatoes are meaty and ripe, but it is also excellent with canned tomatoes, and can be made at any time of the year. And what a great feeling it is to use the stale bread—wasting nothing.

MAKES ABOUT 2 QUARTS, SERVING 8

3 tablespoons extra-virgin olive oil, plus more for the finished *zuppa*

½ cup finely diced yellow onion

6 cloves garlic, crushed and peeled

Three 28-ounce cans whole San Marzano tomatoes

2 cups water

Five ½-inch slices stale Italian bread, crusts removed, cut into 1-1inch cubes

Salt and freshly ground black pepper to taste

10 fresh basil leaves, washed

Freshly grated Grana Padano or Parmigiana-Reggiano cheese

Heat the olive oil over medium heat in a deep, heavy 4-to-5-quart pot. Add the onion and cook until wilted, about 3 minutes. Add the garlic, and cook until golden, about 6 minutes. Meanwhile, crush the tomatoes with your hands or a vegetable mill.

Add the tomatoes and their juice to the pot, add the water, and bring all to a boil, stirring occasionally. Once the tomatoes have boiled for 10 minutes, add the bread to the pot and bring back to a boil. Season lightly with salt and pepper. Add the basil leaves, and adjust the level of heat to maintain a simmer. Cook, uncovered, whisking occasionally to break up the pieces of bread, until the mixture is dense and silky, about 40 minutes.

If desired, remove garlic cloves and basil leaves. Season the soup to taste with additional salt and pepper if needed. Serve in warm bowls, drizzled with extra-virgin olive oil and shreds of fresh basil leaves, and sprinkled with the grated cheese.

PASTA AND BEANS

Pasta e Fagioli

Whether you are Italian or not, you have certainly heard of pasta fazool—every region of Italy (and there are twenty) makes its own version of *pasta e fagioli*, and I would venture to say that every Italian American household has cooked *pasta e fagioli* at one time or other. This soup has the credentials to be the representative dish of Italian cuisine. It's one you must try.

The soup freezes well, but keep in mind that you should cook and add the pasta just before serving.

MAKES 5½ QUARTS, SERVING 12

1 pound dried cannellini (white kidney) beans

6 quarts water

3 large Idaho potatoes (about 1¾ pounds), peeled

3 sprigs fresh rosemary

2 fresh bay leaves, or 3 dried

12 slices bacon, cut crosswise into ½-inch pieces (about 1 cup)

4 cloves garlic, peeled

¼ cup extra-virgin olive oil, plus more for drizzling over the soup

1 medium onion, chopped (between 1 and 1½ cups)

2 medium carrots, peeled and coarsely shredded (about 1 cup)

2 cups canned Italian plum tomatoes (preferably San Marzano), crushed by hand or with a food mill, with their liquid

Salt and freshly ground black pepper to taste

1 pound ditalini, or 3 cups elbow pasta

Freshly grated Grana Padano or Parmigiano-Reggiano cheese

Cold-soak the beans in advance: Dump them into a 2-to-3-quart container, and pour in enough cold water to cover them by at least 4 inches. Let soak in a cool place at least 8 hours or up to 24 hours. Drain well.

Pour the 6 quarts water into a tall, large (at least 10-quart) pot. Add the drained beans, potatoes, rosemary, and bay leaves. Bring to a rolling boil over high heat, then adjust the heat to maintain a gentle boil. Let cook while preparing the sautéed vegetables.

Process the bacon and garlic to a paste in a food processor, stopping once or twice to scrape down the sides of the bowl. Heat the oil in a large skillet over medium heat, then scrape in the bacon-garlic paste and cook, stirring, until golden, about 5 minutes. Stir in the onion and cook, stirring, until translucent, about 4 minutes. Stir in the carrots and cook until the onion begins to brown, about 5 minutes. Add the crushed tomatoes, bring to a boil, then lower the heat and simmer for 5 minutes.

Pour two ladlefuls of the bean-cooking water into the skillet and bring to a boil, then pour the contents of the skillet back into the soup pot. Season lightly with salt and pepper, and bring to a slow boil. Cook until the beans are tender, 45 minutes to 1 hour.

Ladle about one-third of the beans, along with

enough cooking liquid to cover them, into a baking dish or other shallow container where they will cool quickly. Let the beans sit until no longer steaming. (Wait until the beans cool completely before blending or processing; hot beans can cause splatters. If you must, you can stir the beans a bit to speed up the cooling process.) Process the beans and liquid in a food processor or blender until creamy. Return the puréed beans to the pot.

Fish out the potatoes to a plate, mash them coarsely with a fork, and return them to the pot. Cook the soup another 10 minutes to give the flavors a chance to blend. Let the soup rest off the heat, covered, 10 to 15 minutes.

While the soup is resting, cook the ditalini or elbow pasta in salted water until very *al dente*. Drain thoroughly, and stir into the soup. Let all rest for 5 minutes, then serve in warm soup bowls, with a drizzle of extra-virgin olive oil and a sprinkle of Grana Padano or Parmigiano-Reggiano.

MINESTRONE, VEGETARIAN OR WITH PORK

Minestrone Vegetariano o con Maiale

A vegetable soup for Italians is something more than the basic *pasta e fagioli* recipe: the vegetables will be chosen to follow the seasons, and hence the soup will be different every time you make it; for example, asparagus soups are best in the spring, and soups with broccoli best in the winter. This is a basic recipe, but do feel free to substitute your favorite vegetables.

MAKES ABOUT 2 QUARTS, SERVING 8

1 cup dried cannellini, kidney, or Great Northern beans, or chickpeas

About 1½ pounds smoked pork shoulder butt, in 1 piece (optional)

3 tablespoons extra-virgin olive oil

1 medium onion, chopped (about 1½ cups)

Salt, preferably sea salt

2 cloves garlic, finely chopped

One 14-ounce can Italian plum tomatoes (preferably San Marzano)

1 teaspoon hot red pepper flakes

2 fresh bay leaves, or 3 dried

1 large Idaho potato, peeled and cut into ½-inch dice (about 1½ cups)

1 cup ¼-inch slices peeled carrots

½ cup ¼-inch slices peeled celery, with leaves

4 cups shredded green cabbage (1 medium-size cabbage head)

5 quarts hot water

2 small zucchini, trimmed and cut into ½-inch dice (about 1½ cups)

¾ cup ditalini or other small pasta shape, such as tubettini

Freshly ground black pepper to taste

Freshly grated Grana Padano or Parmigiano-Reggiano cheese

Fast-soak the dried beans: Place them in a large saucepan of cold water. Bring to a boil, add the smoked pork if using, cover the pot, and remove it from the heat. Let stand 1 hour.

Heat the olive oil in a large, heavy pot over medium heat. Add the onion, season it lightly with salt, and cook, stirring occasionally, until wilted, about 4 minutes. Add the garlic, and continue cooking until the onion is golden, about 5 minutes.

Use your hands to coarsely crush the tomatoes. Add the crushed tomatoes and their liquid, the hot red pepper, and bay leaves to the pot, and bring to a boil. Add the potato, carrots, and celery, bring to a boil, and cook 5 minutes. Season lightly with salt, then stir in the cabbage and let simmer for 5 minutes.

Pour the hot water into the pot and bring to a boil. Adjust the heat to a gentle boil and cook for 20 minutes. Drain the beans and pork and add them to the pot,

(recipe continues)

tucking the pork into the vegetables so it is completely submerged. Bring the soup to a rolling boil, adjust the heat to a simmer, and cook, covered, until the beans are tender, about 1½ hours. Add the zucchini and cook until softened, about 4 minutes. Remove the pork from the soup, and let stand on a cutting board. Stir the pasta into the soup and cook, stirring occasionally, until *al dente*—tender but firm—about 8 minutes.

Taste the soup, seasoning with salt and pepper if necessary. Let rest off the heat for 5 minutes. While the soup is resting, cut the pork into ½-inch slices and tent them with aluminum foil to keep them warm. When ready to serve, lay a slice of smoked pork in the bottom of each warm soup bowl and ladle the soup over it. Sprinkle with grated cheese and serve.

ESCAROLE AND WHITE BEAN SOUP

Zuppa di Scarola e Cannellini

A southern-Italian specialty, this soup has been a favorite of Italian American immigrants through the generations and still is. It is easy to make, delicious, nutritious, and affordable—all the elements appreciated by those who brought it to this country, and by all of us today who make it in their honor.

SERVES 6

1½ cups dried cannellini, Great Northern, baby lima, or other small white beans

2 quarts water

2 fresh bay leaves, or 3 dried

½ cup extra-virgin olive oil, plus more for drizzling over the finished soup

Salt to taste

6 cups (approximately 1 head) coarsely shredded escarole leaves (preferably the tough outer leaves), washed and drained

8 cloves garlic, peeled and cut in half

4 to 6 whole dried peperoncini (hot red peppers)

Garlic Bread (optional; see page 20)

Cold-soak the beans a few hours in advance: Dump them into a 2-to-3-quart container and pour in enough cold water to cover them by at least 4 inches. Let soak in a cool place for at least 8 hours or up to 24 hours. Drain thoroughly.

Transfer the beans to a large stockpot. Pour in the 2 quarts water, toss in the bay leaves, and bring to a boil. Adjust the heat to maintain a simmer, pour in half of the olive oil, and cook until the beans are tender and only an inch of liquid remains, 1 to 1½ hours. Season the beans to taste with salt, then stir in the escarole, and cook, stirring occasionally, until the escarole is quite tender, about 15 minutes. Remove the pot from the heat.

Heat the remaining olive oil in a small skillet over medium heat. Add the garlic and peppers, and cook, shaking the pan, until the peppers change color, about 1 minute or less. Remove from the heat, and carefully—it will sputter quite a bit—pour one ladleful of soup into the skillet. Swirl the pan to blend everything, and then stir the panful of seasoned soup back into the large pot. Check the seasoning, and let the soup rest off the heat, covered, 10 to 15 minutes. Serve with garlic bread if you like.

WEDDING SOUP

Minestra Maritata

Minestra maritata hails from Basilicata, the region in southern Italy to which I dedicated a whole chapter in *Lidia Cooks from the Heart of Italy*. Everyone who has even the slightest bit of Italian heritage has enjoyed wedding soup (though not always at a wedding). It should be no surprise that many other cultures have similar soups of vegetables and little meatballs—such soups always have a special place at the table. This is one of my favorites, and with some crusty bread it can become a complete meal.

MAKES ABOUT 5 QUARTS, SERVING 12

FOR THE VEGETABLE SOUP

1 medium onion, cut into chunks

2 medium stalks celery with leaves, cut into chunks

1 small carrot, cut into chunks

4 plump cloves garlic, peeled

½ cup loosely packed fresh basil leaves

⅓ cup extra-virgin olive oil

7 quarts cold water

1 head escarole (about 1 pound), cut into ½-inch shreds

1 bunch Swiss chard (about 1 pound), cut into ½-inch shreds

1 large fennel bulb (about 1 pound), trimmed and sliced ¼ inch thick

1 pound zucchini, cut into ½-inch pieces (about 3 small zucchini)

2 tablespoons kosher salt

FOR THE MEATBALLS

4 ounces stale country bread, crusts removed (about 3 or 4 slices)

½ cup milk, or more as needed

1 pound sweet Italian sausage (without fennel seeds)

1 large egg, beaten

½ teaspoon kosher salt

Freshly ground black pepper to taste

2 tablespoons chopped fresh Italian parsley, plus more for serving

Freshly grated pecorino cheese (or half pecorino and half Grana Padano or Parmigiano-Reggiano), plus more for passing

Best-quality extra-virgin olive oil for drizzling

Using the food processor, pulse the onion, celery, carrot, garlic, and basil until they form a smooth paste, or *pestata*. Heat the ⅓ cup olive oil in a large soup pot over high heat, and scrape in the *pestata*. Cook, stirring, until the *pestata* has dried out and just begins to stick to the bottom of the pan, about 5 minutes. Pour the cold water into the pot, stir well, then cover and bring to a boil. Lower the heat, and simmer the broth for about 15 minutes, blending the flavors; then stir in the greens, fennel, zucchini, and salt. Return to a simmer, and cook, covered, for

45 minutes or so, until the greens are tender. Remove the cover, and cook at an active simmer for another 45 minutes or longer, until the soup has reduced a bit in volume and the flavors are concentrated.

While the soup simmers, prepare the meatballs: Tear the bread into chunks, put them in a small bowl, and pour in just enough milk to cover them. Let soak until completely saturated, then lift the bread out of the bowl and squeeze out the milk with your fists. Tear the moistened bread into shreds, and toss them into a large bowl.

Remove the sausage meat from the casing, and crumble it into the shredded bread, breaking up any clumps with your fingers. Pour the beaten egg over the meat, and sprinkle the salt, freshly ground black pepper, and parsley on top. Fold and toss and squeeze all the ingredients through your fingers to distribute them evenly. Scoop up a small amount of the meat mix—about a heaping teaspoon—and roll it in your palms to form a 1-inch ball (the size of a large grape). Continue to form balls until all the meat is used up.

Meanwhile, fill a 4-quart saucepan with 3 quarts of lightly salted water to poach the meatballs, and bring it to a boil. Drop in the meatballs, cover the pot, and return the water to a boil quickly. Adjust the heat to keep the water simmering gently, and poach the meatballs, uncovered, about 5 minutes, until cooked through. Lift them out with a spider or strainer, let drain briefly, and drop them into the finished soup. Bring the soup to a simmer, and cook meatballs and soup together for about 5 minutes.

Ladle the soup into warm bowls. Sprinkle each serving with parsley and some of the grated cheese, and give it a drizzle of your best olive oil. Serve right away, passing more cheese at the table.

SANDWICHES AND PIZZA

SAUSAGE, EGG, AND PEPPERS BREAKFAST SUB

Panino con Frittata di Peperoni e Salsiccia

I just love a good sandwich. Biting into crispy bread that is filled with warm, deliciously cooked food is so incredibly satisfying. This recipe makes a great frittata as well; sausage and peppers is an Italian American classic, and this is the breakfast version, in case you can't wait until lunch.

MAKES TWO 6-INCH SUBS, OR 4 ROLLS

2 tablespoons extra-virgin olive oil

2 links sweet Italian sausage, removed from casing (about 8 ounces)

1 medium onion, thinly sliced

1 large red bell pepper, cored and seeded, sliced ½ inch thick

¾ teaspoon kosher salt

4 large eggs

Two 6-inch lengths Italian bread, or 4 crusty rolls, split and toasted

Heat the oil in a large nonstick skillet over medium heat. When the oil is hot, cook the sausage, crumbling with a wooden spoon, until it is no longer pink, about 3 minutes. Add the onion and bell pepper, season with ½ teaspoon salt, cover, and cook until the vegetables are wilted and lightly caramelized, about 10 minutes.

Beat the eggs with the remaining salt in a small bowl. When the peppers and onions are wilted, pour the eggs into skillet and cook until the eggs are just set but still a little wet, about 1 to 2 minutes. Remove from heat. (The eggs will finish cooking in the pan.)

Mound the frittata on the bread or rolls, and serve immediately.

ASPARAGUS, ONION, AND EGG SANDWICH

Panino con Frittata di Asparagi e Cipolla

Wild asparagus, which I foraged as a child, is more bitter (and thinner) than the farmed variety, but I love any fresh asparagus in this spring frittata. Other vegetables in season—such as mushrooms, broccoli rabe, peppers, and zucchini—can be substituted as well. When I was a child, this sandwich was often taken out to the fields during spring planting for the *merenda* or snack (although the bread does get a bit soggy and it is best eaten immediately).

MAKES 2 HERO SANDWICHES, OR 4 ROLLS

3 tablespoons extra-virgin olive oil

1 medium onion, thinly sliced

½ bunch asparagus, peeled and cut into 2-inch lengths

½ teaspoon kosher salt

4 large eggs

4 ounces mild provola cheese, shredded

Two 6-inch lengths semolina bread, or 4 crusty rolls, lightly toasted

Heat the oil in a large skillet over medium heat, and add the onion, asparagus, and ¼ cup water. Season with ¼ teaspoon of the salt, then cover and let simmer until the water has boiled away and the asparagus is tender, about 10 minutes.

Beat the eggs with the remaining salt. Pour the eggs into the skillet over the vegetables, and cook, stirring, until just beginning to set but still wet, about 1 minute. Sprinkle with the shredded provola, then cover and cook until the cheese melts, about 1 minute more. Uncover, stir to mix the cheese into the omelette, and serve on the toasted bread or rolls.

PIZZA DOUGH

Impasto per la Pizza

You don't need me to tell you why I would include pizza among my favorite recipes. Everyone loves pizza: some like it thin and really crisp, others doughy and chewy. The most important element in making pizza is the dough, and in this recipe I give you instructions to make it all in one day, though I like to let my dough rise slowly in the refrigerator overnight. My favorite pizza is Margherita, with just tomato, mozzarella, and basil, but sometimes I get a craving to add slices of prosciutto, and then toss some fresh arugula on top just before serving it.

MAKES ENOUGH DOUGH FOR 2 PIZZAS OR A BATCH OF 18 SMALL CALZONES

1 package active dry yeast (2¼ teaspoons)

1 teaspoon sugar

6 cups all-purpose flour, plus more for the work surface

1 teaspoon kosher salt

Olive oil for the bowl

Heat 2 cups water to between 90 and 110 degrees F. Stir in the yeast and sugar until dissolved; let sit until foamy, about 5 minutes.

Combine the yeast mixture, flour, and salt in an electric mixer fitted with the paddle attachment. Mix at medium speed until the dough comes together. Switch to your dough-hook attachment. Increase speed to medium-high, and mix until the dough comes together into a smooth mass, about 2 to 3 minutes. The dough will not clear the sides of the work bowl at this point, but should not be too wet. Add a little more water or flour as necessary to get the right consistency, springy to the touch.

Scrape the dough onto a floured work surface and knead several times, until the dough comes together in a smooth ball. Oil a large bowl, then turn the dough in the bowl until it is coated with the oil. Cover with plastic wrap, and let rise until doubled, about 1 to 1½ hours. Punch down the dough and divide in half or into eighteen pieces for calzones.

PIZZA MARGHERITA

Pizza Margherita

In my travels researching *Lidia's Italy in America*, I encountered many different kinds of pizza across America, such as deep-dish in Chicago, a crackerlike pizza in St. Louis, and the classic New York pizza pie. Pizza in Italy is quite different: it's usually a small pie serving one individual, often made with bufala mozzarella—crisp in most regions of Italy, but with a chewy crust in Naples. I enjoy my pizza most with a thin, crispy crust and bufala mozzarella, as in this recipe I've given you, but the fun of pizza is trying all types.

MAKES 2 PIZZAS

1 batch pizza dough (preceding recipe)
½ to ¾ cup Marinara Sauce (see page 102)
4 ounces fresh mozzarella, thinly sliced
1 tablespoon extra-virgin olive oil

Preheat oven to 450 degrees F. Place a pizza stone on the rack in the lower third of the oven. (You can use a sheet pan or a 10-inch cast-iron skillet to bake the pizza if you do not have a stone.)

Divide the dough in half, then form each half into a flat round and let rest on top of your knuckles on both raised fists. Use your knuckles to pull out and stretch the round into a thin circle. Place the dough circle on your work surface, and press it out as thin as you can with your fingertips.

Place the dough circle on a piece of parchment on a pizza peel-paddle (or, if you do not have a pizza paddle, slide the parchment paper with the pizza-dough circle onto the back of a sheet pan). Spread half of the sauce on the dough, using just enough sauce to dot about half of the pizza's surface, leaving a lip around the edge. In the spaces where you haven't dotted sauce, lay half of the cheese. Drizzle with half of the olive oil. Slide off the pizza peel or sheet pan onto the baking stone (or onto your cast-iron skillet).

Bake the pizza until the cheese is melted and bubbly and the crust is browned and crisp on the bottom, about 10 minutes. Remove from oven, and repeat with remaining dough, sauce, cheese, and olive oil.

Pizza Stone
A pizza stone is usually a rectangular stone made of terra-cotta—it helps in baking a good crusty pizza and focaccia, because it heats to high temperature and disperses the heat evenly, cooking the bottom of the pizza evenly and crisply. A pizza stone should not be washed, since it is porous—just scrape and brush off any remaining debris.

PRIMI

Pastas, Polentas, and Risottos

SPAGHETTINI WITH OIL AND GARLIC

Spaghettini Aglio e Olio

This is the quintessential Italian pasta: just about everyone in Italy knows how to make it and loves it. It is one of those magical dishes whose ingredients can be pulled out of the cupboard and turned into a glorious meal in about 15 minutes. In all its simplicity, or maybe because of its simplicity, it is a favorite of many, and makes regular appearances at my table.

SERVES 6

Salt for pasta pot and to taste

1 pound spaghettini or vermicelli

5 tablespoons extra-virgin olive oil

10 cloves garlic, peeled and sliced

½ teaspoon hot red pepper flakes, or more to taste

½ cup chopped fresh Italian parsley

1 cup freshly grated Grana Padano or Parmigiano-Reggiano cheese (optional)

Bring a pot of salted water to a boil over high heat. Stir the spaghettini into the boiling water. Return to a boil, stirring frequently, and cook, semi-covered, until the pasta is tender but still very firm, about 6 minutes.

Meanwhile, heat 3 tablespoons of the olive oil in a large skillet over medium heat. Add the garlic, and cook, shaking the skillet, until pale golden, about 2 minutes. Remove from the heat, and add the crushed hot red pepper. Ladle about 1½ cups of the pasta-cooking water into the sauce; then add the parsley, the remaining olive oil, and salt to taste, and bring to a boil.

Fish out the pasta with a large wire skimmer and drop it directly into the sauce in the skillet. Bring the sauce and pasta to a simmer, tossing to coat pasta with sauce. Cook about 1 minute. Remove the pot from the heat, and toss in the grated cheese if using. Check the seasoning, adding salt and crushed red pepper if necessary. Serve immediately in warm bowls.

SPAGHETTI WITH QUICK GARLIC-TOMATO SAUCE

Spaghetti alla Salsetta Veloce d'Aglio

This is the perfect quick sauce for summer months, or whenever you have some extra canned tomatoes around. By the time the spaghetti cooks, the sauce is done, and will taste very fresh. Honestly, as simple as it is, I love making this recipe—it is one of my favorites because it needs so little yet delivers so much flavor.

SERVES 6

1 teaspoon coarse sea salt or kosher salt, plus 1 tablespoon for the pasta pot

1 pound spaghetti

½ cup extra-virgin olive oil

⅓ cup sliced garlic

4 cups (or a 35-ounce can) canned Italian plum tomatoes (preferably San Marzano), with their liquid, crushed by hand or through a food mill

¼ cup shredded fresh basil leaves (10 large leaves)

Heat the pasta-cooking water—at least 6 quarts water and 1 tablespoon salt—to a boil.

Pour ⅓ cup of the olive oil into a large skillet set over medium-high heat. Scatter in the sliced garlic, and cook until lightly colored. Pour in the crushed tomatoes; rinse the tomato containers with a bit of water, and pour this into the skillet as well. Sprinkle on the teaspoon salt, stir well, and bring to a boil. Cook, stirring occasionally, maintaining a steady boil.

Drop the spaghetti into the cooking water when the tomatoes are perking along. Cook until *al dente*, drain, and drop it into the sauce. Toss the spaghetti and tomatoes for a minute or two, until the pasta is perfectly cooked and dressed.

Turn off the heat, scatter the basil over the pasta, and drizzle on the remaining olive oil. Toss well, and serve immediately.

PENNE WITH CHERRY TOMATOES, BASIL, AND MOZZARELLA

Penne alla Caprese in Crudo

This is one of those pasta dishes where there is no need to cook the sauce—just get the best perfectly ripened tomatoes, the freshest mozzarella, and the most aromatic basil you can find. These ingredients will make the perfect dressing for pasta, especially on hot summer days—rather than weighing down the stomach, this pasta becomes a refreshing and tasty treat. Keeping good ingredients like these on hand means that throwing together a great dinner at the last minute is a breeze.

SERVES 6

1 pound ripe and juicy cherry tomatoes (the ones sold still on the vine are the best), rinsed, dried, and cut in half

¼ cup extra-virgin olive oil, plus more for drizzling over the finished pasta if you like

1 teaspoon sea salt, preferably coarse

Pinch of hot red pepper flakes

4 cloves garlic, peeled

1 pound penne pasta

10 fresh basil leaves, shredded

½ pound bocconcini (bite-size fresh mozzarella), cut in half

Toss the tomatoes, oil, sea salt, and red pepper flakes together in a large bowl. Whack the garlic with the side of a knife, and toss it into the bowl. Let marinate at room temperature, tossing once or twice, for 30 minutes.

While the tomatoes are marinating, bring 6 quarts of salted water to a boil in an 8-quart pot over high heat. Stir the penne into the boiling water, and cook, semi-covered, stirring occasionally, until *al dente*, 10 to 12 minutes.

Remove the garlic from the marinated tomatoes, if you like, and toss in the basil. Drain the pasta, add it to the bowl of tomatoes, and toss well to mix. Check the seasoning, adding salt and more red pepper flakes if necessary. Gently stir in the bocconcini and serve.

SPAGHETTI AND MEATBALLS

Spaghetti con Polpette di Carne

This is one of the most popular and recognized Italian dishes in America, but it is not eaten in Italy. Strange, you might say; but this dish evolved from the kitchens of the early Italian immigrants in America. It has become one of the favorite recipes in *Lidia's Family Table*. Here in America, meat was abundant, unlike in Italy, so on Sunday, the day when families gather at the table, the sauce for the spaghetti was enriched with meatballs. What more can I say, except for *mangia*!

SERVES 6

FOR THE SAUCE

Two 35-ounce cans Italian plum tomatoes (preferably San Marzano), with their liquid

¼ cup extra-virgin olive oil

1 medium onion, chopped (about 1 cup)

1 teaspoon hot red pepper flakes

2 fresh bay leaves, or 3 dried

Kosher salt and freshly ground black pepper, to taste

FOR THE MEATBALLS

½ pound ground pork

½ pound ground beef

1 cup fine dry breadcrumbs

1 cup freshly grated Grana Padano or Parmigiano-Reggiano cheese

¼ cup chopped fresh Italian parsley

2 cloves garlic, peeled and finely chopped

1 large egg

1 teaspoon salt

¼ teaspoon freshly ground black pepper

All-purpose flour for dredging

¼ cup olive oil

¼ cup vegetable oil

1 pound spaghetti

Pass the tomatoes and their liquid through a food mill fitted with the fine disc, or crush by hand. Heat ¼ cup olive oil in a 4-to-5-quart pot over medium heat. Stir in the onion, and cook, stirring, until wilted, about 4 minutes. Pour in the tomatoes, add the crushed red pepper and bay leaves, and season lightly with salt and pepper. Bring to a boil, then lower the heat so the sauce is at a lively simmer. Cook, stirring occasionally, for 30 minutes.

Crumble the pork and beef into a mixing bowl. Sprinkle the breadcrumbs, ⅓ cup grated cheese, the parsley, and garlic over the meat. Beat the egg with the salt and pepper in a small bowl until blended, then pour over the meat mixture. Mix the ingredients with clean hands just until evenly blended, and shape the meat mixture into 1½-inch balls. Dredge the meatballs in the flour until lightly but evenly coated.

Heat ¼ cup olive oil and the vegetable oil in a

large, heavy skillet over medium-high heat. Slip as many meatballs into the skillet as will fit without crowding. Fry, turning as necessary, until golden brown on all sides, about 6 minutes. Adjust the heat as the meatballs cook to prevent them from overbrowning. Remove the meatballs, and repeat if necessary with the remaining meatballs. Add the browned meatballs to the tomato sauce, and cook, stirring gently with a wooden spoon, until no trace of pink remains at the center of the meatballs, about 30 minutes.

Bring 6 quarts of salted water to a boil in an 8-quart pot over high heat. Stir the spaghetti into the boiling water. Return to a boil, stirring frequently. Cook the pasta, semi-covered, stirring occasionally, until done, about 8 minutes. Drain the pasta, and return it to the empty pot. Spoon in about 2 cups of the tomato sauce, tossing well until the pasta is coated with sauce. Remove from the heat, and toss in the remaining ⅔ cup grated cheese. Check the seasoning, and add salt and pepper if necessary.

Serve the pasta in warm bowls or piled high on a large warm platter. Spoon a little more of the sauce over the pasta, and pass the remaining sauce separately. Pass the meatballs family-style in a bowl, or top the bowls or platter of spaghetti with them.

ZITI WITH BROCCOLI RABE AND SAUSAGE

Ziti con Broccoli di Rabe e Salsicce

Broccoli rabe and sausage seem like a marriage made in heaven. They go well together with pasta or on a loaf of Italian bread. The broccoli and sausage pieces get into the crevices of the pasta, and when they're served on bread, the olive oil is immediately soaked up. Even though the bitter and unfamiliar broccoli rabe might not have been an American favorite a few decades ago, when it first appeared in California's Salinas Valley, it certainly has become a favorite ingredient for Italians and Americans today.

SERVES 4

¼ cup olive oil

3 large cloves garlic, crushed and peeled

¼ teaspoon salt, plus 1 tablespoon for the pasta water

1 pound ziti

½ pound sweet Italian sausage, meat removed from casings and crumbled

2 pounds broccoli rabe, cleaned and cut

¼ teaspoon hot red pepper flakes

½ cup grated Grana Padano or Parmigiano-Reggiano cheese

Heat the olive oil in a large, deep, heavy skillet with a fitted lid, then toss in the garlic and sauté, uncovered, until golden, about 2 minutes.

Bring a large pot of salted water to a rolling boil. When you are ready, and the water is boiling, add the ziti to the pot and cook until *al dente*.

Meanwhile, add the sausage meat to the oil and garlic, and cook, stirring, until golden, about 5 minutes. Add the broccoli rabe, 1 cup pasta-boiling water, ¼ teaspoon salt, and the pepper flakes; cover, and steam 5 minutes, stirring occasionally.

Cook the sauce uncovered over high heat for about 3 minutes, until the liquids are slightly reduced. Drain the pasta, add it to the sauce, and toss gently. Sprinkle on half of the cheese, toss again, and distribute the remaining cheese over the pasta. Serve immediately.

TAGLIATELLE WITH WILD MUSHROOM SAUCE

Tagliatelle con Salsa di Funghi

This simple but delicious sauce is best made with fresh porcini, but it would be almost as good with other seasonal fresh mushrooms. Such wild or exotic mushrooms as morels, shiitakes, chanterelles, or any mix can be substituted for all or part of the porcini. I have found that people are passionate about their love of mushrooms: the complex, musty flavors and aromas; the toothsome texture they can have, almost like a piece of meat; and the rich, sensuous taste they add to any dish.

SERVES 6

Salt for the pasta pot, plus more to taste

3 tablespoons extra-virgin olive oil

4 cloves garlic, lightly crushed and peeled

1½ pounds fresh porcini, cleaned, trimmed, and sliced

4 fresh sage leaves

1 cup chicken stock or canned chicken broth

3 tablespoons unsalted butter

Freshly ground black pepper to taste

1½ pounds fresh or dry tagliatelle

3 tablespoons chopped fresh Italian parsley

½ cup grated Grana Padano or Parmigiano-Reggiano cheese

Bring 6 quarts of salted water to a boil for the pasta.

Heat the olive oil in a large skillet over medium heat. Add the garlic, and cook until golden, about 2 minutes. Toss the mushrooms with the sage leaves in the skillet to coat them in the hot oil, and sauté, stirring occasionally, until the mushrooms' liquid has been released and evaporated, about 10 minutes. Pour the chicken stock and butter into the skillet, and let simmer over medium heat until the butter is incorporated into the sauce, about 3 minutes. Add salt and pepper to taste.

Slip the tagliatelle into the boiling pasta water and cook until *al dente*. Drain them well, and return them to the empty pot, now set over low heat. Add the sauce and parsley, and toss gently until the pasta is coated. Remove from heat, add half of the grated cheese, and toss well. Transfer the pasta to a serving platter or individual bowls, and serve immediately with the remaining cheese on hand.

SHELLS WITH YOUNG PEAS AND MUSHROOMS

Conchiglie con Piselli e Funghi

I love using shells for this simple sauce, because the shells collect the peas and the mushroom sauce in the nooks and crannies and deliver a surprise with every forkful. Prosciutto can be substituted for the bacon to give a more authentically Italian taste, and other seasonal vegetables can be added or substituted, as long as they are cut into small pieces to nestle inside the shells.

SERVES 6

Salt for the pasta pot, plus more to taste

1½ cups shelled young peas or frozen baby peas

2 tablespoons extra-virgin olive oil

2 slices bacon, finely chopped

½ cup chopped spring onions or scallions

2 cups cleaned and sliced mixed mushrooms, such as shiitake, oyster, and crimini

2 cups chicken stock or canned chicken broth

1 tablespoon unsalted butter

Freshly ground black pepper to taste

1 pound small pasta shells (conchiglie)

½ cup freshly grated Grana Padano or Parmigiano-Reggiano cheese

Bring a large pot of salted water to a boil for the pasta.

If using fresh peas, blanch them in a medium saucepan of boiling water 2 minutes. Drain the peas, and rinse them under cold water until cool. Drain them thoroughly. (Frozen peas need to be defrosted and drained, but not blanched.)

Heat the olive oil in a large skillet over medium heat. Add the bacon and onions, and sauté, stirring, until the onions are wilted, about 4 minutes. Add the mushrooms, and sprinkle them with salt. Continue to cook, stirring occasionally, until all the mushrooms have released and lost their moisture, about 5 minutes.

Pour in the chicken stock, peas, and butter, and season the entire pan lightly with salt and pepper. Simmer until the liquid is reduced by half, about 10 minutes. Check the seasoning, and adjust if necessary.

Meanwhile, stir the shells into the boiling pasta water. Cook the pasta, stirring occasionally, until *al dente*—tender but firm—about 12 minutes.

Drain the pasta, and return it to the empty pot, now set over low heat. Pour in the sauce, and stir over low heat until the pasta is coated. Remove from heat, and add the grated cheese. Toss well, and transfer to a warmed serving platter or individual bowls.

VERMICELLI WITH RED CLAM SAUCE

Vermicelli con le Vongole Salsa Rossa

Pasta with clam sauce is my grandchildren's favorite, and I get no greater enjoyment than watching them slurp down the pasta with the juicy clam sauce. Vermicelli, a type of very thin spaghetti, cooks as quickly as the clams do, so have your ingredients ready and the water boiling when you are ready to start cooking the sauce.

SERVES 6

3½ pounds littleneck clams

½ teaspoon coarse sea salt or kosher salt, or to taste, plus salt for the pasta pot

10 tablespoons extra-virgin olive oil, plus more if needed

10 cloves garlic, peeled and sliced

½ teaspoon hot red pepper flakes

1 cup tomatoes al filetto—fresh or canned plum tomatoes, seeded and sliced in thin strips

4 tablespoons chopped fresh Italian parsley

1 pound vermicelli

Put the clams in a single layer on a tray or platter, and freeze them for about ½ hour. (Slightly frozen clams are easier to open.)

Working over a bowl to catch every drop of clam liquid, open the clams with a shucking knife, cut the meat free from both half-shells, and let the meat and liquid fall into the bowl. Reserve 8 of the smaller clams. Collect the clam meat from the bowl and strain the juice through a sieve set over a small bowl or measuring cup. Let the sediment in the clam juice settle, then pour off the clean clam juice from the top into a clean bowl, discarding the sediments. Chop the clams roughly into large pieces.

Before starting the sauce, bring a large pot of water to a boil for the pasta—4 quarts water with 1 tablespoon salt.

Pour ½ cup of the olive oil into a large skillet, and set over medium-high heat. Scatter in the sliced garlic and the reserved whole clams, heat to sizzling, and sprinkle the hot red pepper flakes over it. Cook another minute, add the sliced tomatoes and the reserved clam liquid, stir, and bring to the boil. Cook for 2 to 3 minutes, and stir in the chopped clams. Return to a boil, and cook at a bubbling simmer for 3 or 4 minutes—if the clams release a frothy scum, scoop it off the surface and discard. When the sauce has achieved a nice density, just enough to coat a spoon lightly, lower the heat and season with salt to taste. Stir in the parsley and another 2 tablespoons of olive oil.

When you add the clam juice, drop the vermicelli in the boiling water. Cook briefly, 2 to 4 minutes, then lift the pasta from the pot, using a spider or tongs—it will still be quite *al dente*. Let it drain briefly, and drop it into the simmering sauce. Toss the vermicelli in the sauce for a couple of minutes, until the pasta is cooked through and dressed with the sauce. Serve immediately.

LOBSTER FRA DIAVOLO WITH SPAGHETTI

Aragosta Fra Diavolo con Spaghetti

Just about everybody loves lobster, but in this preparation the flavor and meat of the lobster go a long way. The preparation requires space and attention in the kitchen, but once it is on the table, everybody rolls up their sleeves, and digging in comes naturally. It is a pasta and main course all in one. Make sure you put extra empty bowls on the table for the shells, and extra napkins for the hands and face. Keep in mind it is *fra diavolo*, meaning spicy; if you prefer the sauce on the mild side, just reduce or omit the peperoncino.

SERVES 6

Three 1¼-to-1½-pound live lobsters (I recommend Maine lobsters)

Salt for the pasta pot

1 pound spaghetti

1½ cups vegetable oil, or as needed

1½ cups all-purpose flour

¼ cup extra-virgin olive oil

8 cloves garlic, peeled

Two 35-ounce cans Italian plum tomatoes (preferably San Marzano), with their liquid, passed through a food mill or crushed by hand

8 whole dried peperoncino or diavollilo hot red peppers, or 1 teaspoon crushed hot red pepper flakes

1 teaspoon dried oregano, preferably the Sicilian or Greek type dried on the branch, crumbled

1 teaspoon chopped fresh oregano

½ teaspoon kosher salt

Place the lobsters in the freezer about 30 minutes before beginning the recipe. (This will make it easier to take them apart.)

Bring a large pot of salted water to a boil over high heat for the pasta.

Remove the lobsters from the freezer, and start by cutting off their claws and legs with a sturdy pair of kitchen shears. Whack the claws with a meat mallet just hard enough to crack the shells, and use the shears to cut along one side of the joints attached to the claws. (Cracking the claws and cutting the joints will make it easier to remove the meat from the shell after the lobster is cooked.)

Lay each lobster on a cutting board with the tail stretched out, and cut in half lengthwise by inserting a heavy, sharp knife where the tail meets the head section. Holding the tail firmly as you cut, bring the knife down to the cutting board in a swift motion, cutting the body cleanly in half. Turn the knife in the other direction, and cut the tail in half in the same way. Open up the cut lobster, and remove the antennae and eyes with the shears, making sure to scrape out the digestive sac located inside the shell behind the eyes. Pull out the dark vein that runs along the tail, but leave the tomalley—the pale-green mass in the head close to the tail—intact. (It adds wonderful flavor to the sauce.)

Heat 1 cup of the vegetable oil in a wide, heavy skillet over medium heat. Dredge the meat side of the bodies in flour, patting lightly with fingers so it will adhere to the lobster. When the skillet of oil is hot, add the floured lobster quarters cut side down; continue adding as many as will fit comfortably in the skillet. Cook until the lobster meat is lightly browned, about 5 or 6 minutes. Remove from the pan, and repeat with the remaining lobster pieces, if necessary, adding more vegetable oil to the pan as needed. When all the lobster bodies have been lightly browned, add the claws to the pan, and cook, turning them with tongs, until the shells turn bright red on all sides, about 4 minutes. (Turn the lobster pieces carefully—they are likely to splatter.)

Heat the olive oil in a wide, deep braising pan large enough to hold all the lobster pieces, over medium heat. Whack the garlic cloves with the side of a knife, and add them, along with the small lobster legs, to the oil. Cook, shaking the pan, until the garlic is lightly browned, about 3 minutes. Pour in the crushed tomatoes; add the peppers and dried oregano, and season lightly with salt. Bring the sauce to a boil, and adjust the heat to a lively simmer for 10 minutes.

Meanwhile, stir the spaghetti into the boiling water. Cook, stirring frequently, until done, about 6 minutes.

Stir in the fresh oregano, and tuck all the lobster pieces into the sauce skillet. Cook at a lively simmer just until the lobster meat is cooked through and juicy, about 5 minutes. If the sauce becomes too dense as it simmers, ladle a little of the pasta-cooking water into the pan. Keep the sauce and lobster warm over very low heat.

Drain the spaghetti, and return it to the empty pot. With a ladle, spoon the liquid portion of the lobster sauce over the pasta, leaving just enough sauce behind in the pan to keep the lobster pieces moist. Bring the sauce and pasta to a boil, stirring gently to coat the pasta with sauce. Check the seasoning, adding salt if necessary.

Divide the dressed spaghetti among six pasta bowls. Top each with half a lobster body, tail, and one claw. Spoon some of the sauce remaining in the pan over each serving, and serve immediately.

ZITI WITH ROASTED EGGPLANT AND RICOTTA CHEESE

Ziti alla Norma

This is a delicious Sicilian pasta dish, and as I discovered in Palermo, while researching *Lidia's Italy*, found on just about every restaurant menu there. In Sicily they fry the eggplant cubes before they add them to the pasta, but here I instruct you to bake the eggplant—it is just as good, but with much less fat. I am asked for this recipe over and over again—my viewers seem to love eggplant, as well as ricotta, and this dish is the perfect marriage of the two.

SERVES 6

2 large, firm eggplants (each about 3 inches in diameter and 1¼ pounds)

2 tablespoons coarse salt, plus more for cooking the pasta and seasoning the sauce

6 tablespoons extra-virgin olive oil

2 cloves garlic, peeled and sliced

One 35-ounce can Italian plum tomatoes (preferably San Marzano), with their liquid, crushed by hand

1 teaspoon hot red pepper flakes

1 pound ziti

1 cup freshly grated Grana Padano or Parmigiano-Reggiano cheese

1 cup fresh basil leaves, washed, dried, and shredded

½ pound (1 cup) whole-milk ricotta

Trim the stems from the eggplants. Remove strips of peel about 1 inch wide from the eggplants, leaving about half the peel intact. Cut the eggplants into 1-inch cubes, and toss in a large bowl with the 2 tablespoons salt. Dump into a colander, and let drain for 1 hour. Rinse the eggplant under cool running water, drain thoroughly, and pat dry.

Preheat the oven to 400 degrees F. Brush a baking sheet with half the olive oil. Turn the eggplant cubes onto the baking sheet, toss to coat with oil, and spread them out in an even layer. Bake until the eggplant is very tender and browned, about 25 minutes. Turn and stir the eggplant cubes gently once or twice during baking so they cook evenly.

Bring a large pot of salted water to a boil over high heat for the ziti.

Heat the remaining olive oil in a large skillet over medium heat. Scatter the garlic over the oil, and cook, shaking the pan, until golden, about 3 minutes. Pour in the crushed tomatoes, add the pepper flakes, and season lightly with salt. Bring to a boil, then reduce the heat and simmer for 10 minutes.

(recipe continues)

Stir the ziti into the boiling water. Return to a boil, stirring frequently. Cook the pasta, semi-covered, stirring occasionally, until *al dente*, about 10 minutes.

Drain the pasta, and return it to the empty pot over low heat. Pour in about half of the sauce, tossing lightly to coat the pasta with sauce. Remove the pot from the heat, stir in ½ cup of the grated cheese and the basil. Toss in half of the roasted eggplant cubes and toss again, then add the ricotta by heaping tea-spoonfuls, stirring it gently into the pasta; you want the ricotta to warm, but you do not want it to blend with the sauce completely.

Plate the pasta, and spoon the reserved sauce over each serving. Now add equal amounts of the remaining baked eggplant to the top of all the pasta plates. Sprinkle with the remaining grated cheese, and serve.

ZITI WITH SAUSAGE, ONIONS, AND FENNEL

Ziti con Salsicce, Cipolla, e Finocchio

This meaty *sugo,* or skillet sauce, cooks at a leisurely pace, while a few ingredients are creating a rich and complex sauce. In the first few minutes, you want to caramelize each ingredient as it is introduced to the pan—this is especially important with the tomato paste, to give it a good toasting before it is diluted with the pasta water. The sauce needs 6 minutes or more at a good bubbling simmer after adding the water, in order to draw out and meld the flavors of the meat and vegetables, as well as to soften the pieces of fresh fennel.

SERVES 6

Salt for the pasta water

1 pound ziti

1 pound sweet Italian sausage (without fennel seeds)

1 large fennel bulb (about 1 pound)

⅓ cup extra-virgin olive oil

2 medium onions, cut into half-moon slices (about 2 cups)

½ teaspoon salt

½ teaspoon hot red pepper flakes

½ cup tomato paste

⅓ cup finely chopped fennel fronds

1 cup freshly grated pecorino (or Grana Padano or Parmigiano-Reggiano) cheese

Heat a large pot of salted water to boiling for the pasta. Drop the ziti into the boiling water, then bring back to a boil and cook until the ziti are not quite *al dente.* Drain, reserving 3 cups of the pasta water.

While the pasta is cooking, remove the sausage from its casing and break the meat up a bit with your fingers. Trim the fennel bulb, removing any tough outer parts, reserving the fronds. Slice the bulb in half lengthwise, remove core, then slice each half in ¼-inch-thick lengthwise slices. Separate the slivers of fennel if they are attached at the bottom; cut the long slivers in half so you have about 3 cups of 2-inch-long matchsticks of fennel. Heat the olive oil in a skillet set over medium-high heat. Add the sausage meat, and cook, stirring and breaking it up more with a wooden spoon, until it sizzles and begins to brown, about 1½ minutes. Push the sausage to the sides of the pan, and drop the onion slices into the clear part of the pan; sauté, stirring, until they sizzle and wilt, another 2 minutes or so, then stir them in with the meat. Clear a new space, and drop in the

(recipe continues)

fennel; let it heat up and wilt for 1 minute or more, then stir to combine.

Sprinkle on ¼ teaspoon salt; drop the hot red pepper flakes into a cleared hot spot, and toast the flakes for 30 seconds, then stir to combine. Clear a good-sized hot spot in the center of the pan, plop in the tomato paste, and cook, stirring it in the spot, for a good minute or more, until it is sizzling and caramelizing; then stir it in with everything else.

Ladle the reserved pasta water into the skillet, stir well, and bring the liquid to a boil. Reduce to a simmer, and let cook until the flavors have developed,

the sauce is thickened but not too thick, and the fennel is soft but not mushy, 6 minutes or more. (Add more water if the sauce reduces too rapidly.) Season to taste.

Drop the cooked ziti into the simmering sauce. Toss everything together, then sprinkle over it the chopped fennel fronds, and continue to cook until the ziti are perfectly *al dente* and coated with sauce.

Remove the skillet from the heat, sprinkle the grated cheese over the ziti, and toss it in. Serve the hot pasta right from the skillet into warm pasta bowls.

BAKED STUFFED SHELLS

Conchiglie Ripiene al Forno

The whole family loves this recipe, and it is a great dish to make when you have lots of guests coming for dinner. Once you've stuffed the shells and set them in the baking dish, the rest is easy. The delicious aroma will fill the house while your guests are having drinks, and the shells will arrive bubbling hot to the table. Let's face it, everyone loves baked pasta—the chef and the guests.

SERVES 6
(ABOUT 5 STUFFED SHELLS PER PERSON)

1½ pounds whole-milk ricotta

One 35-ounce can peeled Italian plum tomatoes (preferably San Marzano)

Salt and freshly ground white pepper to taste

1 pound fresh mozzarella cheese

1 cup freshly grated Grana Padano or Parmigiano-Reggiano cheese

⅓ cup chopped fresh Italian parsley

1 large egg

¼ cup extra-virgin olive oil

6 cloves garlic, peeled and crushed

½ teaspoon hot red pepper flakes

10 fresh basil leaves

1 pound jumbo pasta shells

Place the ricotta in a cheesecloth-lined sieve, and set the sieve over a bowl, allowing any liquid to drip out. Discard the liquid in the bowl.

Pass the tomatoes through a food mill fitted with the fine disk. (If you don't have a food mill, place them in a food processor, using quick on/off pulses until finely ground. Don't overprocess, or you'll incorporate air into the tomatoes and change their texture and color.) Bring a pot of salted water to a boil over high heat for the pasta.

Slice half the mozzarella thin, and cut the remaining half into ¼-inch cubes. Turn the drained ricotta into a mixing bowl, and stir in the mozzarella cubes, grated cheese, and parsley. Season to taste with salt and white pepper. Beat the egg well, and stir it into the ricotta mixture.

Heat the olive oil in a large skillet over medium heat. Scatter the garlic over the oil, and cook, shaking the pan, until golden brown, about 2 minutes. Carefully pour the tomatoes into the skillet. Add the crushed red pepper, and season lightly with salt. Bring the sauce to a quick boil, then adjust the heat to keep it simmering. Cook until the sauce is lightly thickened, about 30 minutes. Stir the basil into the sauce a few minutes before it is done.

Preheat the oven to 425 degrees F.

Stir the shells into the boiling salted water, and cook, semi-covered, stirring occasionally, until slightly firmer than *al dente*, about 7 minutes. Fish the shells out of the water with a large skimmer, and carefully lower them into a bowl of cold water. Let cool, then drain carefully.

Line the bottom of a 10-by-15-inch baking

dish with about ¾ cup of the tomato sauce. Spoon about 2 tablespoons of the ricotta mixture into each shell—the shell should be filled to capacity, but not overstuffed. Nestle the shells next to one another in the baking dish as you fill them. Spoon the remaining sauce over the shells, coating each one. Arrange the slices of mozzarella in an even layer over the shells. Bake until the mozzarella is browned and bubbling, about 25 minutes. Remove, and let stand 5 minutes before serving.

SPAGHETTI IN TOMATO APPLE SAUCE

Spaghetti al Sugo di Pomodoro e Mele

Tomato-and-apple sauce might sound odd to you, but not so in Trentino–Alto Adige, one of the most northerly regions of Italy, known for its delicious apples. While researching for *Lidia Cooks from the Heart of Italy*, I ended up climbing an apple tree in Trentino–Alto Adige to harvest the perfect apples for this recipe. What fun, and I admit I ate a few while I was up the tree.

SERVES 6

3 cups canned Italian plum tomatoes (preferably San Marzano)

6 tablespoons extra-virgin olive oil

2 large stalks celery, cut into ¼-inch dice (about 1 cup)

1 medium onion, chopped (about 1 cup)

1 teaspoon kosher salt, plus more for the pasta pot

1 pound tart and firm apples, such as Granny Smith

1 pound spaghetti

1 cup freshly grated Grana Padano or Parmigiano-Reggiano cheese, plus more for passing

Pour the canned tomatoes into a food processor or blender, and purée until smooth.

Pour 4 tablespoons of the olive oil into a skillet, set it over medium heat, and strew the celery and onion in the pan. Cook and stir the vegetables for about 5 minutes, until they wilt and start to caramelize.

Stir in the puréed tomatoes, season with the salt, and heat to a bubbling simmer. Cook, stirring occasionally, for 5 minutes or so. As the tomatoes perk, peel and core the apples, and remove the seeds. Shred them, using the coarse holes of a shredder or grater.

When the tomatoes have cooked about 5 minutes, stir the apples into the sauce. Bring the skillet back to a simmer, and cook the sauce, uncovered, for about 15 minutes, stirring now and then, until it has reduced and thickened and the apple shreds are cooked and tender.

Meanwhile, bring a large pot of salted water to a rolling boil, drop in the spaghetti, and cook it until just *al dente*. Lift the spaghetti from the water, let drain for a moment, and drop it into the warm sauce. (Reheat if necessary.)

Toss the pasta with the sauce for a minute or two, until all the strands are coated and perfectly *al dente*. Turn off the heat, sprinkle the grated cheese over the pasta, and toss well. Drizzle over it the remaining olive oil, toss once again, and heap the pasta in warm bowls. Serve immediately, passing more cheese at the table.

SPAGHETTI AND PESTO TRAPANESE

Pesto alla Trapanese

Pesto has become very familiar in American homes by now—that is, pesto made with fresh basil leaves, garlic, and pignoli nuts. Well, this one is different—it is an uncooked sauce freshly flavored with herbs, almonds, and tomatoes. It is a recipe I discovered in Sicily while researching for *Lidia's Italy*, and I have received countless e-mails about this recipe, praising its simplicity and rich flavor. I am sure it will become one of your favorites.

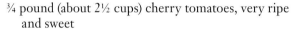

SERVES 4 TO 6

¾ pound (about 2½ cups) cherry tomatoes, very ripe and sweet

12 large fresh basil leaves

1 plump clove garlic, crushed and peeled

⅓ cup whole almonds, lightly toasted

¼ teaspoon hot red pepper flakes, or to taste

½ teaspoon coarse sea salt or kosher salt, or to taste, plus more for the pasta pot

½ cup extra-virgin olive oil

1 pound spaghetti

½ cup freshly grated Grana Padano or Parmigiano-Reggiano cheese

Rinse the cherry tomatoes and basil leaves, and pat them dry. Drop the tomatoes into a blender jar or food-processor bowl, followed by the basil leaves, garlic clove, the almonds, hot red pepper flakes, and ½ teaspoon salt. Blend for a minute or more to a fine purée; scrape down the bowl, and blend again if any large bits or pieces have survived. With the machine still running, pour in the olive oil in a steady stream, emulsifying the purée into a thick pesto. Taste, and adjust seasoning. (If you're going to dress the pasta within a couple of hours, leave the pesto at room temperature. Refrigerate it for longer storage, up to 2 days, but let it return to room temperature before cooking the pasta.)

To cook the spaghetti, heat 6 quarts of water, with 1 tablespoon salt, to the boil in a large pot. Slip in the spaghetti, and cook until *al dente*.

Scrape all the pesto into a big warm bowl. Lift the cooked spaghetti up, drain briefly, and drop directly into the pesto. Toss quickly to coat the spaghetti, sprinkle the cheese all over, and toss again. Serve immediately in warm bowls.

STRAW AND HAY

Paglia e Fieno

This colorful pasta dish has been on restaurant menus as far back as I can remember. Patrons love the two-tone pasta, crispy peas, prosciutto bits, and creamy sauce. Your family and guests will ask for second helpings every time. But, as traditional as this dish is, feel free to change the vegetables according to seasons; for example, I love adding fava beans in the spring, corn in the summer, mushrooms in the fall, and cooked chestnuts in the winter.

SERVES 6

Salt for the pasta pot

4 scallions

2 tablespoons extra-virgin olive oil

1 cup shelled fresh peas, blanched, or frozen baby peas, defrosted

6 to 8 slices imported prosciutto, cut crosswise into ½-inch-thick ribbons

⅔ cup chicken stock or canned low-sodium chicken broth

½ cup heavy cream

1 pound fresh *paglia e fieno* fettuccine, or ½ pound dry egg fettucine and ½ pound dry spinach fettuccine

¾ cup freshly grated Grana Padano or Parmigiano-Reggiano cheese

Bring a large pot of salted water to a boil over high heat.

Trim the roots, tips, and any yellow or wilted leaves from the scallions. Cut them in half lengthwise, then crosswise into 3-inch lengths. Cut the scallion pieces lengthwise into thin strips.

Heat the oil in a large, heavy skillet over medium heat. Add the scallions, and cook until wilted, 1 to 2 minutes. Scatter in the peas and cook until just tender, about 3 minutes. Add the prosciutto, and toss until it changes color, 1 to 2 minutes. Pour in the chicken stock, and bring the liquid to a boil. Reduce the sauce to a simmer, and cook until the liquid is reduced by half. Add the heavy cream, and continue to simmer until the liquid is lightly thickened, 2 to 3 minutes.

Stir the pasta into the salted boiling water. Return to a boil, and cook the pasta until *al dente*. Fish the pasta out of the boiling water with a large wire skimmer, and add it directly to the sauce in the skillet, stirring to coat the pasta with sauce. Cook over high heat until the liquid is reduced enough to form a creamy sauce. Remove from the heat, toss in the grated cheese, and serve immediately in warm bowls.

SPAGHETTI WITH CALAMARI, SCALLOPS, AND SHRIMP

Spaghetti di Tornola

Just about every region that is touching the sea in Italy (fifteen out of twenty regions!) has a version of a seafood sauce to dress a quick plate of pasta. This recipe is from Calabria, which has quite a bit of coast for fishing, and is where the best spicy pasta in Italy can be found. I visited Calabria during my travels for *Lidia Cooks from the Heart of Italy*, and was so happy to bring this dish back with me as a souvenir.

SERVES 6

1 teaspoon kosher salt, plus more for the pasta pot

8 ounces medium calamari, cleaned

8 ounces dry sea scallops

1 pound large shrimp

¼ cup extra-virgin olive oil, plus 2 tablespoons for finishing the pasta

6 plump cloves garlic, peeled and sliced

4 cups cherry tomatoes, halved; or 2 cups canned Italian plum tomatoes (preferably San Marzano), crushed by hand or with a food mill

¼ teaspoon hot red pepper flakes, or to taste

1 pound spaghetti

¼ cup chopped fresh basil leaves

1 tablespoon chopped fresh Italian parsley

Fill a large pot with salted water (at least 6 quarts water, with 1 tablespoon salt), and heat to a boil.

To prepare the seafood: Cut the calamari bodies, including the tentacles, into ½-inch segments. Pull off the side muscle, or "foot," from the scallops, if present, and discard. Remove the shells, tails, and digestive veins from the shrimp; rinse and pat dry.

Heat the olive oil in a skillet set over medium-high heat. Scatter in the sliced garlic, and cook, stirring occasionally, until it begins to sizzle and color, about 1 to 2 minutes. Dump in the cherry tomatoes, sprinkle on the teaspoon salt and the hot red pepper flakes, and cook for about 5 minutes, stirring and tossing the tomatoes, until they are softened and sizzling in their juices but still intact. Now start cooking the pasta first and the seafood right after, so they are ready at the same time.

Drop the spaghetti into the boiling water, stir, and return the water to a boil. As it cooks, scatter the calamari rings and cut tentacles in the pan with the tomatoes, and get them sizzling over medium-high

(recipe continues)

heat. Let the pieces cook for a minute or two, then toss in the scallops, and spread them out to heat and start sizzling quickly. After they've cooked for a couple of minutes, toss in the shrimp, ladle in a cup of boiling pasta water, stir the seafood and sauce together, bring to a steady simmer, and cook just until the shrimp turn pink and begin to curl, about 3 minutes.

As soon as the spaghetti is barely *al dente*, lift it from the pot, drain briefly, and drop into the skillet. Toss the pasta and the simmering sauce together for a minute or two, until the spaghetti is nicely coated with sauce and perfectly *al dente*, and the seafood is distributed throughout the pasta. Turn off the heat, sprinkle on the basil and parsley, and drizzle on another 2 tablespoons olive oil. Toss well, heap the spaghetti into warm bowls, giving each portion plenty of seafood, and serve immediately.

BASIC POTATO GNOCCHI
Gnocchi di Patate

Kids love gnocchi. Adults love gnocchi. Even our household pets eat gnocchi (without the cheese, of course). There is something about the warming feeling of satisfaction after eating a plate of delicious gnocchi that makes this little dumpling rank high on everyone's list. Potato gnocchi is something I made often as a child, helping Grandma and Mom prepare what was usually Sunday dinner.

People shy away from making gnocchi, but they are rather simple to make. There are two things to remember: Once you have riced the potatoes, spread them out, and let them cool completely. Do not overknead the dough, but, rather, work it just enough to incorporate the ingredients together.

SERVES 6

6 large Idaho or russet potatoes

2 tablespoons plus 1 teaspoon salt

Dash of freshly ground white pepper

2 eggs, beaten

About 4 cups unbleached all-purpose flour

Grated Grana Padano or Parmigiano-Reggiano cheese for serving (optional)

Boil the potatoes in their skins for about 40 minutes, until easily pierced with a skewer. When cool enough to handle, peel and rice the potatoes, and set them aside to cool completely, spreading them loosely to expose as much surface as possible to air.

Bring 6 quarts of water and 2 tablespoons of the salt to a boil in a large pot. On a cool, preferably marble work surface, gather the cold potatoes into a mound, forming a well in the center. Stir the remaining teaspoon salt and the white pepper into the beaten eggs, and pour the mixture into the well. Work the potatoes and eggs together with both hands, gradually adding 3 cups of the flour and scraping the dough up from the work surface with a knife as often as necessary. (Incorporation of the ingredients should take no longer than 10 minutes—the longer you work it, the more flour it will require and the heavier it will become.)

Dust the dough, your hands, and the work surface lightly with flour and cut the dough into six equal parts. (Continue to dust as long as the dough feels sticky.) Using both hands, roll each piece of dough into a rope ½-inch thick, then slice the ropes at ½-inch intervals. Indent each dumpling with a thumb, or use the tines of a fork to produce a ribbed effect. (This helps the sauce stick to the gnocchi.)

Drop the gnocchi into boiling water a few at a time, stirring gently and continuously with a wooden spoon, and cook for 2 to 3 minutes, until they float up to the surface. Remove the gnocchi from the water with a slotted spoon or skimmer, transfer them to a warm platter, and add a little sauce of your choice. Add freshly ground white pepper to taste and, if appropriate, grated cheese, and serve immediately.

Gnocchi can be delicious with just butter and cheese, or sage-and-butter sauce, or plain Tomato Sauce (see page 103). Or try the next recipe.

GNOCCHI WITH GORGONZOLA AND PEAS

Gnocchi con Piselli e Gorgonzola

There is something very special about the marriage of creamy Gorgonzola and gnocchi, the mellowness and comforting feel of the gnocchi with the pungent Gorgonzola melted on them. A beautiful harmony of flavors.

SERVES 6

Salt for the gnocchi pot

2 tablespoons unsalted butter

½ cup heavy cream

1 cup chicken stock, vegetable stock, or pasta-cooking water

One 10-ounce box frozen peas, thawed

6 ounces Gorgonzola, crumbled

1 batch Basic Potato Gnocchi (see preceding recipe)

¼ cup grated Grana Padano or Parmigiano-Reggiano cheese

Bring a pot of salted water to a boil to cook the gnocchi.

For the sauce, heat a large skillet over medium-high heat. Melt the butter, then add the cream and stock. Once the mixture is simmering, add the peas. Bring to a rapid bubble, and cook until reduced to a sauce, about 5 minutes. Stir in the Gorgonzola until it dissolves in the sauce. Keep the sauce warm while you cook the gnocchi.

Meanwhile, shake excess flour from the gnocchi and add to the boiling water (don't crowd the gnocchi; cook in batches if necessary). Once the gnocchi rise to the surface, simmer until cooked through, about 2 minutes. Remove the gnocchi directly to the sauce with a spider. Toss the gnocchi in the sauce for a minute (add a little pasta water if it seems too tight), just to coat the gnocchi with the sauce, then remove from the heat. Sprinkle with the grated cheese, toss, and serve.

BASIC RISOTTO

Risotto

Making a risotto was considered challenging a few decades back. Now America has mastered the technique and is truly enjoying the versatility of risotto, which can be served alongside seasonal vegetables, beneath a piece of perfectly cooked fish or poultry, or as the main course.

This recipe makes a simple but delicious *risotto alla parmigiana*, but you can flavor it by adding your favorite vegetables, shrimp, or tomato or meat sauce that you might have on hand, or use the recipes that follow. On the other hand, if you want to do something more elaborate, I recommend *risotto alla milanese*, made with saffron and beef marrow, which you can find in *Lidia Cooks from the Heart of Italy.*

SERVES 6

5 to 7 cups of tasty meat or vegetable stock

4 tablespoons extra-virgin olive oil

2 cups (about 10 ounces) fairly finely chopped onion

1 cup chopped shallots

1 teaspoon salt

2 cups short-grain Italian rice, either Arborio or Carnaroli

1 cup white wine

2 tablespoons butter

1½ cups freshly grated Grana Padano or Parmigiano-Reggiano cheese, plus more for the table

Freshly ground black pepper to taste

Pour the stock into a large pot, and bring it almost to a boil. Cover, and keep it hot over very low heat, on a burner close to the risotto pan.

Put the oil, onions, shallots, and half of the salt in a large pan, and set over medium heat. Cook the onions slowly, stirring frequently with a wooden spoon, as they sweat, soften, and gradually take on a golden color, 8 to 10 minutes.

Ladle ½ cup of the hot stock into the onions, stir well, and continue to cook over low to medium heat for another 5 to 10 minutes, by which time the onions should be completely golden and glistening and the stock will have evaporated.

When the onions are completely devoid of stock, add the rice all at once, raise the heat to medium, and stir constantly. Cook for about 3 minutes, until the rice grains have been toasted, but do not allow them to scorch or color.

Pour in the wine all at once, and cook with the rice for 2 to 3 minutes over medium heat. Stir constantly all around the pan until the liquid has been

(recipe continues)

absorbed. Have the hot stock close by, and be ready to add it with a ladle or measuring cup.

For the first addition, ladle in 1½ to 2 cups of the very hot stock, enough to barely cover the rice; stir it in continuously, all around the pan. Add remaining ½ teaspoon of salt, and stir well. Lower the heat, if necessary, to maintain a very gentle perking.

After the addition of at least 5 cups of stock, you can taste and gauge the degree of doneness of the rice kernels and the fluidity of the creamy suspension. Whenever you find the rice grains pleasantly *al dente* and the risotto creamy, you can choose to stop cooking. Or you may incorporate more stock, up to about 7 cups total, if you want a softer, looser risotto. When you are satisfied, turn off the heat.

Stir frequently at first, and then constantly as the risotto thickens. Make sure the spoon is reaching into all the corners of the pan, so everything is constantly being stirred. When all the stock has been absorbed, the risotto is harder to stir (the bubbling sounds thicker, too), and the pan bottom is visible, ladle in another cup of water. (If you are flavoring your risotto with a sauce, stir it in at this point, before the second addition of stock.)

Cook, always stirring, and add another 2 cups of stock when the risotto is ready for it, as just described—anywhere from 3 to 6 minutes between additions. Keep track of how much liquid you have added.

Remove from heat, and stir in the butter. Stir in grated cheese and freshly ground pepper to taste, whisking with a wooden spoon. When it's nice and creamy, serve the risotto immediately in heated bowls, with more grated cheese at the table.

CREAMY RICE WITH "PIGLET" MUSHROOMS

Risotto con Porcini

Porcini are the ideal mushrooms for this risotto, but any mushroom or mixture of mushrooms will yield a delicious risotto. *Porco* is an Italian word for "pig," and porcini have the chubby, oblong shape of the body of a pig—hence the "piglet" mushroom. Typically Italian, this is one of the most common risotto dishes served in the United States. For more details on risotto, see the basic risotto recipe (page 83).

SERVES 4

5 tablespoons olive oil

1 cup minced onion

2 tablespoons minced shallots

12 ounces fresh porcini mushrooms, sliced

2 cups Arborio rice

½ cup dry white wine

6½ cups hot chicken or vegetable stock

½ teaspoon salt

2 tablespoons butter, cut into bits

½ cup freshly grated Grana Padano or Parmigiano-Reggiano cheese

Freshly ground black pepper to taste

Heat the olive oil in a medium casserole, and sauté the onion and shallots until golden. Add the mushrooms, and sauté until tender, about 5 minutes. Add the rice, and stir to coat it with oil. Pour in the wine, stir well, and add ½ cup of the hot stock and the salt. Cook, stirring constantly, until all the liquid has been absorbed. Continue to add hot stock in small batches (just enough to completely moisten the rice), stirring constantly to help the liquid absorb, until the rice mixture is creamy and *al dente*.

Remove from the heat, whip in the butter and cheese, season with pepper to taste, and serve immediately.

RISOTTO WITH VEGETABLES

Risotto con Verdure

When making this risotto, choose any vegetable that is in season. It is a wonderful way of creating exciting new combinations of flavors that will be yours to pass on. It can become a spring pea risotto, an autumn squash risotto, a winter beet risotto, or a summer corn risotto. This risotto is also a wonderful way to use leftover vegetables you might have in the refrigerator or freezer.

SERVES 6

½ pound broccoli (about 1 medium-size stalk)

1 cup blanched fava beans or frozen baby lima beans

½ teaspoon salt, plus more as needed

3 tablespoons extra-virgin olive oil

½ cup minced scallions, greens included (about 6)

1 tablespoon minced shallot

2½ cups Arborio or Carnaroli rice

½ cup dry white wine

6½ cups hot vegetable stock or chicken broth

2 tablespoons unsalted butter, cut into bits

½ cup freshly grated Grana Padano, Parmigiano-Reggiano, or Pecorino Romano cheese

Freshly ground black pepper to taste

Trim the broccoli florets from the stems, keeping them small enough to fit on a spoon. (You should have about 1¼ cups.) Peel the stems with a small knife or vegetable peeler, then cut them into 2-inch pieces. Steam the florets just until bright green, about 1 minute. Steam the stems until very tender, about 4 minutes. Reserve the steaming liquid. Transfer the stems to a blender or food processor, and process until smooth. You will probably have to add some of the steaming liquid to make a smooth mixture. Scrape out the purée into a small bowl, and set the florets and purée aside.

If using the baby lima beans, cook them in a small saucepan of boiling salted water for 2 minutes. Drain them thoroughly and set aside.

Heat the olive oil in a heavy casserole or pot over medium heat. Add the scallions and shallot and sauté until translucent, stirring often, about 4 minutes. Add the rice, and stir to coat with the oil. Toast the rice until the edges become translucent, 1 to 2 minutes.

Pour in the wine, and stir well until evaporated. Add ½ cup of the hot stock and the ½ teaspoon salt. Cook, stirring constantly, until all the stock has

(recipe continues)

been absorbed. Continue to add hot stock in small batches—just enough to completely moisten the rice—and cook until each successive batch has been absorbed. After the risotto has cooked for 12 minutes, stir in the broccoli purée and the favas or limas. About 3 minutes after that, stir in the broccoli florets. Stir constantly, and adjust the level of heat so the rice is simmering very gently while adding the stock, until the rice mixture is creamy but *al dente*. This will take about 18 minutes from the first addition of stock.

Remove the casserole from the heat. Whip in the butter first, until melted, then the grated cheese. Adjust the seasoning with salt, if necessary, and pepper. Serve immediately, ladled into warm shallow bowls.

RICE WITH FRESH SAGE

Riso e Salvia

When you want to enjoy a risotto-style rice but don't have the time for lots of prep and stirring, try this simple recipe. It is great as a main course or a flavorful side dish for grilled chicken and braised meats.

SERVES 6 OR MORE AS A FIRST COURSE
OR SIDE DISH

4 tablespoons butter, plus 2 tablespoons butter cut into pieces for finishing

12 large fresh sage leaves

5 cups hot water or light stock, plus more if needed

2½ teaspoons kosher salt

2 cups Italian short-grain rice, such as Arborio or Carnaroli

1 bunch scallions, finely chopped (about 1 cup), for finishing

½ cup freshly grated Grana Padano or Parmigiano-Reggiano cheese, plus more for passing

Melt the 4 tablespoons butter in a saucepan over medium heat. When the butter is foaming, scatter the sage leaves in the pan and heat for a minute or so, just until they are sizzling. Pour in 5 cups of hot water or stock, and stir in the salt. Raise the heat, and bring the liquid to the boil; then stir in the rice and bring back to the boil.

Cover the pan, and lower the heat so the water is bubbling gently. Cook for 13 or 14 minutes, then check the rice and add more liquid if needed. At this point, too, stir in the scallions, to cook for the last minute or two, until the rice is creamy and *al dente*.

When the rice is fully cooked, turn off the heat, drop in the butter pieces, and stir vigorously until they have completely melted. Stir in the ½ cup of grated cheese, spoon the riso into warm pasta bowls, and serve immediately, passing additional grated cheese at the table.

TRADITIONAL RICE AND CHICKEN

Riso alla Pitocca

Every culture has its rendition of chicken and rice, and this recipe has become one of my most requested dishes; people love rice and people love chicken. Risotto is on everybody's radar these days, and though it's delicious, it does require constant attention. Here is a dish that rivals risotto for flavor but is much simpler to make. My grandmother used to make it often for us, and we all loved it.

SERVES 4 TO 6

1½ pounds boneless, skinless chicken thighs

1 cup onion cut into 1-inch chunks

1 cup carrot cut into 1-inch chunks

1 cup celery cut into 1-inch chunks

2 plump cloves garlic, peeled

½ cup extra-virgin olive oil

1 tablespoon kosher salt

1 fresh bay leaf

1 cup dry white wine

5 cups hot chicken or turkey stock, plus more if needed

2 cups Italian short-grain rice, such as Arborio or Carnaroli

2 tablespoons butter, cut into pieces

3 tablespoons chopped fresh Italian parsley

½ cup grated Grana Padano or Parmigiano-Reggiano cheese, plus more for passing

Trim any excess fat from the chicken thighs, and cut the thighs into 1-inch chunks. Use a food processor to mince the onion, carrot, celery, and garlic into a fine-textured *pestata*.

Pour the olive oil into a saucepan, and set over medium-high heat. Stir in the *pestata*, and season with 1 teaspoon of the salt. Cook for about 5 minutes, stirring frequently, until the *pestata* has dried. Toss in the chicken pieces and the bay leaf, and sprinkle with remaining salt. Tumble the chicken in the pan until browned and caramelized all over, about 4 minutes.

Raise the heat, pour in the white wine, and cook, stirring and scraping up the browned bits in the pan, until the wine has almost completely evaporated. Pour in the hot stock, stirring, and add the rice. Bring to a boil over high heat, then cover and reduce the heat to keep the riso bubbling gently. Cook for about 14 minutes, or until both the rice and the chicken chunks are fully cooked and the consistency is creamy. Turn off the heat, drop in the butter pieces, and stir vigorously until thoroughly amalgamated; then stir in the parsley and ½ cup of grated cheese. Spoon the riso into warm pasta bowls, and serve immediately, passing additional grated cheese at the table.

BASIC POLENTA

Polenta

Corn is a food from the New World—it only came to Italy after the discovery of the Americas. But you could never tell the people from the region of Friuli–Venezia Giulia, the region I hail from, that polenta is not Friulian. In fact, the Friulani are called *polentoni*, "polenta eaters," much as the Tuscans are called *mangiafagioli*, "bean eaters." Corn is a plant that yields a lot of fruit in relation to the land and attention it needs, and since hunger was always prevalent in that area of Italy, corn became a staple to feed the people and the animals. Soon there were daily cauldrons of polenta cooking in the *fogolar*s, the open hearths of Friuli.

SERVES 8

8 cups water, or as needed

2 fresh or dried bay leaves

1 tablespoon coarse salt, or as needed

1 tablespoon extra-virgin olive oil

1½ cups coarse yellow cornmeal

In a small saucepan, bring 4 cups of water to a simmer; keep this "backup" water hot, covered, over medium-low heat. Bring the remaining water, the bay leaves, and 1 tablespoon salt to a boil in a 3-to-4-quart cast-iron saucepan, over medium-high heat. When boiling, add the olive oil.

Scoop up a small handful of the cornmeal, and, while stirring constantly with a wooden spoon or flat-ended stirrer, let it sift slowly through your fingers into the seasoned boiling water. Let the cornmeal fall *a pioggia*—like rain—into the water. Sift the remaining cornmeal into the water a small handful at a time, stirring constantly, paying special attention to stirring the corners of the pot. It should take about 5 minutes to add all the cornmeal.

When all the cornmeal has been added, the mixture should be smooth and thick and begin to "perk," with large bubbles rising to the surface. Reduce the level of heat to medium-low, and continue stirring until the mixture becomes too thick to stir easily, about 4 minutes. Add enough of the "backup"

(recipe continues)

water—about 1 cup—to restore the mixture to a smooth stirring consistency. Stir until the mixture is again too thick to stir easily. Continue adding water and stirring like this until the cornmeal is tender, about 20 minutes after the cornmeal was added.

When the cornmeal is tender, stir the polenta without adding water until it is shiny and begins to gather around the spoon as you stir it, 5 to 10 minutes. (The polenta should be thick enough to stand a spoon in.) The polenta is ready to serve at this point, or you can choose to cook it an extra few minutes to intensify the flavor. To continue cooking, reduce the level of heat to low, and stir the polenta constantly for 5 to 10 minutes. You may need to add a small amount of water during this extra cooking if the polenta begins to stick or become too thick.

Pour the polenta away from you into a ceramic bowl. Let it stand 10 minutes before serving. To serve polenta, scoop it onto plates with a large spoon, dipping the spoon in water before each scoop. (An ice-cream scoop can be used in the same fashion; it makes nice round mounds of polenta.)

Polenta at the Table

FOR IMMEDIATE SERVING: You may also serve the polenta hot directly from a board in the traditional way: Pour the hot polenta into the center of a wooden cutting board, keeping the polenta in a long, high mound. Let the polenta stand a few minutes, until it is firm enough to cut. Cut the polenta with a string stretched taut between your index fingers, or with a thin knife. Gently transfer the slices to plates.

TO CHILL THE POLENTA FOR BAKING, GRILLING, OR PAN-FRYING: You can begin to see the true versatility of polenta when it has been chilled until firm and cut into shapes for baking, grilling, or pan-frying. To serve polenta this way, pour the hot polenta—either freshly made for this purpose, or remaining from a batch made to be eaten hot—into a baking pan or mold to a thickness of about ½ inch. (One whole recipe of Basic Polenta makes enough to fill two 9-by-13-inch baking dishes to a depth of about ½ inch.) Cover with plastic wrap applied directly to the surface, and refrigerate until thoroughly chilled and very firm, 4 to 5 hours. Invert the polenta onto a cutting board and cut it into any desired shape for baking, grilling, or frying.

TO BAKE: Place the polenta pieces on a lightly oiled baking sheet and place in a preheated 375-degree-F oven until lightly browned and crispy, about 20 minutes. Turn the polenta once about halfway through the cooking.

TO GRILL: Lightly brush both sides of the polenta pieces with olive oil. Place on a hot grill, and cook, turning once, until well marked and heated through, about 2 minutes per side.

TO PAN-FRY: Heat a small amount of olive oil in a nonstick skillet over medium-high heat. Add the polenta slices, and cook, turning once, until golden brown and crispy on both sides, 8 to 10 minutes.

BAKED POLENTA LAYERED
WITH MUSHROOM RAGÙ

Polenta Pasticciata ai Funghi

Polenta pasticciata is a layered baked dish, just like lasagna, but made with warm, fresh polenta instead of pasta. And, like lasagna, it is marvelously versatile: you can fill the layers of polenta with all manner of good things—cheeses, vegetables, meats, or sauces, or a combination of everything. People absolutely love it for the complexity of flavor, and because it can be prepared in advance. It is a great family preparation, and I have a rendition of it in *Lidia's Family Table;* it can be made ahead of time, just like lasagna.

SERVES 12, WITH LEFTOVERS
THAT CAN EASILY BE FROZEN

1 batch (about 10 cups) Basic Polenta (preceding recipe), freshly made and hot, with or without freshly grated Grana Padano or Parmigiano-Reggiano cheese (it will be richer if you include it, but just as good without it)

4 to 6 cups Mushroom Ragù (see page 106), Marinara Sauce (see page 102), or Tomato Sauce (see page 103).

2 tablespoons soft butter for the baking dish, or more if needed

1 to 2 cups shredded Muenster or dry-packed mozzarella, Italian Fontina, cheddar, or a soft cheese of your liking

½ to 1 cup grated Grana Padano or Parmigiano-Reggiano cheese

Preheat the oven to 400 degrees F, and set a rack in the center. Make your polenta in a large bowl, then put plastic wrap over the top, to keep it warm and to prevent a skin from forming on top. Be sure to assemble the *pasticciata* within ½ hour, while the polenta is still warm and soft with no lumps.

If necessary, heat the filling sauce to quite warm. If it is too dense for spreading, thin it with some water.

Butter the bottom and sides of a 9-by-13-inch baking dish or a 12-inch cast-iron skillet thoroughly. Use more butter on the bottom, in particular, if you want to unmold the *pasticciata* onto a platter.

Pour in half the polenta (approximately 5 cups), and spread it evenly in the bottom of the pan. Scatter ⅓ cup or more shredded Muenster or other soft cheese all over the top, then sprinkle on 2 to 4 tablespoons of grated Grana Padano or Parmigiano-Reggiano. Pour or ladle 2 cups of the warm sauce over the polenta and

(recipe continues)

cheese, and spread it all over—use 3 cups sauce if you want a thicker layer.

Pour on a bit more than half of the remaining polenta (about 3 cups) and spread it, and top with shredded soft cheese and grated hard cheese in the amounts you like. Pour in the remaining sauce, and spread it evenly, reserving a cup, if you have enough and plan to unmold the *pasticciata*.

For the top layer, spread all the rest of the polenta, and another ¼ cup sauce on top of that. Sprinkle on more shredded soft cheese and grated Grana Padano or Parmigiano-Reggiano. If you're making a thin *pasticciata* in a big pan, or want it to have a beautiful deep-golden crust or *gratinato*, use enough cheese to really cover the top. Do not compress the cheeses, though. (See note below.)

Set the pan on a cookie sheet, and bake for 45 minutes to an hour, or more, until the top is deeply colored and crusted, even browned a bit on the edges. Let the *pasticciata* cool for a few minutes before serving. If serving portions from the baking pan, cut into squares (like lasagna), or wedges if you've used a round skillet or pan, and lift them out with a spatula.

If unmolding the *pasticciata*: Let it cool for at least 10 minutes. Run a knife around the sides of the pan, cutting through any crust sticking to the rim or sides. Lay a big board on top of the baking pan or skillet, hold the two together (with the protection of cloths and the help of other hands if necessary), and flip them over. Rap on the upturned pan bottom—or bang on it all over—to loosen the bottom. Lift the board, and give the pan a good shake. The *pasticciata* will eventually drop out. Serve on the board, or reflip it onto a serving platter, and serve with a cup or more of warm sauce heaped on the top or served on the side.

NOTE If you want to prepare the *pasticciata* and bake later the same or the next day, do not sprinkle the cheese on top. Cover it, wrap it well, and refrigerate. Before baking, sprinkle on the cheeses and make a tent of foil over the baking dish, without touching the cheese. Poke a few small holes in the foil, to vent steam. Set the pan on a sheet, and bake for ½ hour at 400 degrees F; then remove the foil and continue to bake until deeply colored and crusted.

SAUCES

ITALIAN AMERICAN MEAT SAUCE

Sugo di Carne

This sauce has to be a favorite in every Italian American home. If for nothing else, all the love and time that goes into making it puts it high up on the cook's list of favorites. It evokes memories of the Sunday table, all the family gathered around, and the celebrations that bubbled up as you ate together. One of my best Sunday memories is the aroma of the Sunday sauce permeating the house early in the morning, which leads to the memory of laughter at the table. I know many of you share the delightful memory of Sunday sauce with me. The sauce can be prepared entirely in advance and refrigerated for up to 5 days, or frozen for up to 3 months, so any extra sauce will keep well.

MAKES ABOUT 8 CUPS, ENOUGH TO DRESS
ABOUT 2 POUNDS OF PASTA

Two 35-ounce cans Italian plum tomatoes (preferably San Marzano)

¼ cup extra-virgin olive oil

2 medium yellow onions, diced (about 2 cups)

6 to 8 cloves garlic, peeled and finely chopped

5 or 6 meaty pork neck bones (about ¾ pound—ask your butcher to set them aside for you)

1 pound ground beef

1 pound ground pork

½ teaspoon kosher salt

4 fresh bay leaves, or 5 dried

1½ teaspoons dried oregano, preferably the Sicilian or Greek type dried on the branch, crumbled

¾ cup dry white wine

⅓ cup tomato paste

3 to 4 cups hot water

Pass the tomatoes through a food mill fitted with the fine blade. Set aside.

Heat the olive oil in a heavy pot over medium heat. Add the onions, and cook, stirring occasionally, until golden, about 8 minutes. Make room in the center of the pot to add the garlic, and cook until it is lightly browned. Add the pork bones, and cook, turning, until they are lightly browned on all sides, about 5 minutes. Add the ground beef and pork, and season lightly with salt. Cook, stirring to break up the meat, until the liquid it gives off is boiled away, about 10 minutes. Continue cooking until the meat is browned, about 5 minutes. Add the bay leaves and oregano, then pour in the wine. Bring to a boil, and cook, scraping up the brown bits that cling to the pot, until the wine is completely evaporated.

Pour the tomatoes into the pot, then stir in the tomato paste until it is dissolved. Season lightly with salt. Bring to a boil, adjust the heat to maintain a lively simmer, and cook, uncovered, stirring often, 2 to 3 hours. Add the hot water, about ½ cup at a time, to maintain the level of liquid while the sauce cooks. Skim off any fat floating on top, remove pork bones, and adjust the seasoning. Serve over pasta.

MEAT SAUCE BOLOGNESE

Sugo alla Bolognese

Once you have had a truly good Bolognese sauce, it will become one of your go-to recipes. Bolognese is a very versatile sauce: it can dress all shapes and sizes of pasta, whether fresh tagliatelle, dried spaghetti, or baked rigatoni. This recipe makes enough sauce to feed a hungry crowd, but it also freezes well if you want to enjoy it in smaller quantities.

MAKES 6 CUPS, ENOUGH FOR ABOUT
1½ POUNDS DRIED PASTA

3 tablespoons extra-virgin olive oil

1 medium yellow onion, minced (about 1 cup)

1 medium carrot, peeled and finely shredded (about ½ cup)

½ cup minced celery with leaves

Salt

1 pound ground beef

1 pound ground pork

½ cup dry red wine

1 tablespoon tomato paste

3 cups canned Italian plum tomatoes (preferably San Marzano), crushed

3 fresh bay leaves, or 4 dried

Freshly ground black pepper

4 cups hot water, or as needed

Heat the olive oil in a wide 3-to-4-quart pan or Dutch oven over medium heat. Stir in the onion, carrot, and celery, season them lightly with salt, and cook, stirring, until the onion is translucent. Crumble in the ground beef and pork, and continue cooking, stirring to break up the meat, until all the liquid the meat has given off has evaporated and the meat is lightly browned, about 10 minutes. Pour in the wine, and cook, scraping the bottom of the pan, until the wine is evaporated, 3 to 4 minutes. Stir in the tomato paste, and cook a few minutes; then pour in the tomatoes, toss in the bay leaves, and season lightly with salt and pepper.

Bring to a boil, then lower the heat so the sauce is bubbling. Cook, stirring occasionally, until the sauce is dense but juicy and a rich dark-red color. This will take about 2 to 3 hours—the longer you cook it, the better it will become. While the sauce is cooking, add hot water as necessary to keep the meats and vegetables covered.

CLASSIC PESTO

Pesto alla Genovese

Pesto has now become a household sauce: it is easy to make, and its freshness of flavor has made it an often found friend on American tables. Pesto is at its best when used immediately after it is made, though it can be refrigerated for up to a few weeks if it's spooned into a container, topped with olive oil, and sealed tight. If you find yourself with an abundance of basil in summer, make some pesto and store it in small portions in the freezer, where it will last for up to a few months. (Frozen pesto gives a great burst of fresh flavor to hearty winter soups and pasta sauces.) I've given you two methods for how to make this, with a mortar and pestle or with a food processor, but the results either way are delicious.

**MAKES ABOUT ¾ CUP,
ENOUGH FOR I POUND PASTA**

4 cups loosely packed fresh basil leaves (about 60 small or 30 large fresh basil leaves), gently washed and dried

Pinch of coarse sea salt

2 cloves garlic, peeled

3 tablespoons pine nuts, lightly toasted

2 tablespoons freshly and finely grated Pecorino Romano cheese

2 tablespoons freshly and finely grated Grana Padano or Parmigiano-Reggiano cheese

3 to 4 tablespoons extra-virgin olive oil

To make the pesto in a mortar: Place a few leaves of the basil in the bottom of a mortar, and sprinkle the salt over them. Crush the leaves coarsely with the pestle, add a few more leaves, and continue crushing, adding new leaves each time those in the mortar are crushed, until all the leaves are coarsely ground. Toss in the garlic, and pound until the mixture forms a smooth paste. Add the pine nuts, and grind them to a paste. Stir in the cheeses, then enough of the olive oil to give the pesto a creamy consistency.

To make the pesto in a food processor: Combine the basil, salt, and garlic in the food processor, add 2 tablespoons of the oil, and blend at low speed, stopping frequently to press the basil down around the blades, until a coarse paste forms. Toss in the pine nuts, and pour in the remaining olive oil. Blend until the pine nuts are finely ground. Stir in the grated cheeses to form a creamy paste.

MARINARA SAUCE

Salsa Marinara

Canned plum tomatoes make an easy and delicious marinara sauce. You can make this sauce with fresh tomatoes as well, but I recommend doing it only when the juiciest, most flavorful ripe tomatoes are available.

MAKES ABOUT 1 QUART,
ENOUGH FOR 6 SERVINGS OF PASTA

¼ cup extra-virgin olive oil

8 cloves garlic, peeled

One 35-ounce can Italian plum tomatoes (preferably San Marzano), lightly crushed, with their liquid

Salt and hot red pepper flakes to taste

10 fresh basil leaves, torn into small pieces

Heat the oil in a 2-to-3-quart nonreactive saucepan over medium heat. Whack the garlic with the flat side of a knife, add it to the oil, and cook until lightly browned.

Carefully slide the tomatoes and their liquid into the oil. Bring to a boil, and season lightly with salt and red pepper flakes. Lower the heat so the sauce is at a lively simmer, and cook, breaking up the tomatoes with a whisk or spoon, until the sauce is chunky and thick, about 20 minutes. Stir in the basil about 5 minutes before the sauce is finished. Taste the sauce, and season with salt and red pepper if necessary.

TOMATO SAUCE

Salsa di Pomodoro

There is a light version of tomato sauce, just tomatoes, garlic, and olive oil, quickly cooked with some added basil. The tomato sauce in this recipe is longer-cooking, with vegetables added to it, making it more complex in flavor.

MAKES ABOUT I QUART,
ENOUGH FOR 6 SERVINGS OF PASTA

¼ cup extra-virgin olive oil

1 small onion, chopped (about ⅓ cup)

¼ cup finely shredded peeled carrots

¼ cup finely chopped celery (including leaves)

Two 35-ounce cans peeled Italian tomatoes (preferably San Marzano), seeded and lightly crushed, by hand or with a food mill, with their liquid

4 fresh bay leaves, or 2 dried

Salt and hot red pepper flakes to taste

Heat the oil in a 2-to-3-quart nonreactive saucepan over medium heat. Stir in the onion, and cook, stirring occasionally, until wilted, about 3 minutes. Add the carrots and celery, and cook, stirring occasionally, until golden, about 10 minutes.

Add the crushed tomatoes and bay leaves, and bring to a boil. Season lightly with salt and red pepper. Lower the heat so the sauce is at a lively simmer, and cook, stirring occasionally, until thickened, about 45 minutes. Remove the bay leaves. Taste, and season with salt and red pepper if necessary.

BUTTER AND SAGE SAUCE

Salsa di Burro e Salvia

This is a delicious and simple sauce, but intense with sage flavor, and perfect for dressing gnocchi. It's delicious even when just lightly drizzled over fresh grilled fish or poultry—a little is all you need. You can find this simple recipe mostly in the north of Italy, where fresh pasta prevails, but today even the Roman *trattorie* serve it.

MAKES ABOUT I CUP,
ENOUGH FOR I POUND PASTA

1½ sticks butter (12 tablespoons), or more to taste

10 whole fresh sage leaves

1 cup hot water from the cooking pot of your pasta of choice

¼ teaspoon freshly ground black pepper, or to taste

1 cup Grana Padano or Parmigiano-Reggiano cheese, grated

Melt the butter in a sauté pan over medium heat until just foaming. Gently lay the sage leaves in the pan, and heat until the leaves crisp up, about a minute

Ladle in 1 cup boiling pasta water; stir the sauce, and simmer for about 2 minutes, reducing liquid by half. Grind the black pepper directly into the sauce.

Keep the sauce hot over very low heat; return to a simmer, and immediately add cooked pasta to the sauce. Toss with the sauce, then remove from heat, and sprinkle with the cheese just before serving.

MUSHROOM RAGÙ

Ragù di Funghi Misti

This is a great vegetarian sauce, very complex and satisfying. It's excellent for pasta, baked in a lasagna or *polenta pasticciata*, cooked into risotto—or as a condiment for grilled steak or fish. The mushrooms you can buy at the supermarket will make a fine sauce, but if you have fresh wild mushrooms it will be even better. In either case, dried porcini provide the key flavor in this sauce. It is a sauce that freezes well, so freeze whatever extra you may have made.

MAKES ABOUT 6 CUPS,
ENOUGH FOR 3 POUNDS PASTA

½ ounce dried porcini (about ½ cup loosely packed pieces), soaked in 1½ cups warm water for a few minutes, until reconstituted

2½ pounds small, firm, fresh mixed mushrooms

3 sprigs fresh thyme

1 sprig fresh rosemary, a tender stem about 4 inches long

1 sprig fresh sage with 4 big leaves or more smaller ones

¼ cup extra-virgin olive oil

4 tablespoons butter

1 medium onion, finely chopped (about 1 cup)

1 cup finely chopped shallots

½ teaspoon salt, plus more to taste

⅓ cup tomato paste

1 cup dry Marsala

4 cups hot chicken or vegetable stock

Freshly ground black pepper

Squeeze out the soaked porcini, and slice them into pieces about ¼ inch wide. Strain the soaking water, and keep it in a warm spot. Clean, trim, and slice the fresh mushrooms into moderately thin slices, barely ¼ inch wide. Tie the sprigs of fresh herbs together with a piece of kitchen twine, or enclose the leaves in cheesecloth.

Put the oil and butter in a large skillet, and place over medium heat. When the butter melts, dump in the onion and shallots and half the salt, and stir well. Heat to a slow sizzle, and cook for 6 minutes or more, stirring often, until the onions are soft, wilted, and shiny, without any browning.

Pour all the mushrooms into the pan, and spread them out. Sprinkle in the remaining salt, drop in the herb bouquet, then toss briefly and cover the pan. Raise the heat a bit, and cook, covered, for about 3 minutes, shaking the pan now and then to sweat the mushrooms.

Uncover, and continue to cook over fairly high heat, stirring frequently, as the mushrooms shrink and the liquid evaporates, 5 minutes or more. When the pan is dry and the mushrooms begin to brown, clear a spot, drop in the tomato paste, and toast it, stirring, for a minute or so; then stir it into the mushrooms.

When everything is browning again and just starting to stick, pour the Marsala all over. Stir constantly as the wine thickens and evaporates. When the mushrooms again start sticking to the bottom, pour in the warm mushroom water and 2 cups of the hot stock. Bring to an active boil, stirring up any caramelization on the pan bottom. Lower the heat to keep the sauce bubbling gently all over the surface, and cover the pan. Cook for about 20 minutes, occasionally stirring and adding stock to keep the mushrooms nearly covered in liquid; expect to add ½ cup or so at a time. Adjust the heat to keep the sauce simmering.

Uncover the pan, and cook for another 20 minutes, continuing to simmer the ragù and adding stock as needed. When the mushrooms are thoroughly tender and the sauce has just thickened, remove and discard the herb bouquet. Season with salt and freshly ground black pepper to taste.

RAW SUMMER TOMATO SAUCE FOR PASTA

Salsa Cruda di Pomodoro

This recipe requires ripe and juicy homegrown tomatoes or heirloom tomatoes from the farmers' market. Be sure to have them at room temperature, for the sauce actually develops in the hour or two that it marinates: salt draws the juices from the tomatoes, and they become infused with the flavors of basil and garlic. Then all you do is toss piping-hot pasta with the tomatoes and enjoy a rare treat of summer.

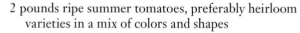

MAKES 3 TO 4 CUPS,
ENOUGH FOR 1 POUND PASTA

2 pounds ripe summer tomatoes, preferably heirloom varieties in a mix of colors and shapes

3 to 4 plump cloves garlic, peeled

½ teaspoon salt

6 large basil leaves

¼ teaspoon hot red pepper flakes, or more or less to taste

½ cup extra-virgin olive oil

1 cup or more grated Grana Padano or Parmigiano-Reggiano or cubed fresh mozzarella cheese (optional)

Rinse the tomatoes, drain, and wipe dry. Cut out the core and any other tough parts. Working over a big mixing bowl to catch all the juices, cut the tomatoes—cherry tomatoes in half; regular tomatoes into 1-inch chunks—and drop them into the bowl.

Smash the garlic cloves with a chef's knife, and chop into a fine paste (easier if you add some of the salt as you chop; mash the garlic bits and salt with the flat side of the knife, too). Scatter the garlic paste and the rest of the salt (½ teaspoon in all) over the tomatoes, and stir gently. Pile up the basil leaves, and cut into thin strips; you should get about 3 tablespoons. Scatter these over the tomatoes, then sprinkle in the hot red pepper flakes. Pour in the oil, stir, and fold, to coat the tomatoes and distribute the seasonings.

Cover the bowl with plastic wrap, and let it marinate at room temperature for 1 to 2 hours.

Toss the marinated sauce with freshly cooked and drained pasta. Serve as is, or toss in 1 cup grated Grana Padano or Parmigiano-Reggiano. For extra richness, add 1 cup or more cubed fresh mozzarella.

SIDES
AND VEGETABLES

SMOTHERED ESCAROLE

Scarola Affogata

Italians love their bitter greens, like chicory, kale, and, of course, escarole. When my family first came to America, escarole was always on the table—it was readily available, affordable, and a good source of nutrition. And, when prepared this way, it always reminded us of home. But this simple Italian recipe applies well to the preparation of most green leafy vegetables, such as spinach, kale, and broccoli rabe.

SERVES 4

1 pound (approximately 2 medium heads) escarole

6 cloves garlic, crushed and peeled

3 tablespoons olive oil

½ teaspoon salt

¼ teaspoon hot red pepper flakes

Freshly ground black pepper

To prepare the escarole, cut out the core, wash the leaves twice in abundant cold water, drain, and discard any damaged or discolored leaves. Sauté the garlic in oil in a large pot until golden but not brown. Add the leaves and seasonings, cover, and cook over moderate heat 3 or 4 minutes, stirring occasionally. Remove and discard the garlic; serve immediately.

SWISS CHARD POTATOES

Bietola e Patate

Swiss chard has only recently become a popular vegetable in the United States, but I grew up on it and loved it, and this was my favorite way of cooking it. Chard can be found with beautifully colored stems, which really adds to the presentation of this dish. Traditionally we used regular potatoes, but now I sometimes replace them with sweet potatoes.

This dish is especially good when made in advance and reheated.

SERVES 6

2 pounds Swiss chard

4 quarts salted water

3 medium Idaho potatoes (about 1¼ pounds), peeled and cut crosswise into 4 pieces

¼ cup extra-virgin olive oil

4 cloves garlic, crushed and peeled

Salt and freshly ground black pepper

To prepare the chard: Trim the ends from the stems. Cut off and discard any wilted or yellow parts of the leaves. Strip the stems from the leaves, and cut the stems into ½-inch lengths. Cut the leaves in half lengthwise, then crosswise into ½-inch strips. Wash the leaf and stem pieces thoroughly, then drain them well.

Bring the salted water to a boil in a large pot. Add the potatoes, and cook 20 minutes, until tender. Add the Swiss chard stems. After another 10 minutes add the leaves, then cook all until the vegetables are very tender, an additional 5 minutes. Drain in a colander.

Heat 2 tablespoons of the olive oil in a large skillet over medium heat. Add the garlic, and cook just until it begins to brown, about 1 minute. Add the Swiss chard and potatoes, and season them lightly with salt and pepper. Cook, stirring and mashing the potatoes, until the liquid is evaporated and the potatoes are coarsely mashed. If the potatoes begin to brown, adjust the level of heat to medium-low and continue stirring. Add the remaining 2 tablespoons olive oil, and season to taste with salt and pepper, stir, and serve hot.

OLIVE OIL MASHED POTATOES

Pure di Patate all'Olio

Who doesn't like mashed potatoes? Of course we love them, but everyone wants to be careful about adding too much butter. So try making it the way my *nonna* used to make it in Italy—with olive oil, or with garlic and olive oil. It's healthier, and still a favorite at our table. For a variation, toast three garlic cloves in olive oil in a large skillet and add to the riced or mashed potatoes.

SERVES 4

1 pound Idaho or Yukon Gold potatoes, scrubbed but unpeeled

Salt

¼ cup extra-virgin olive oil

Freshly ground pepper, preferably white

Pour enough cold water over the potatoes in a large saucepan to cover them by a few inches. Season the water with salt, and bring to a boil. Cook until the potatoes are tender but still hold their shape, 15 to 30 minutes, depending on the size and shape of the potatoes. Drain the potatoes, and let stand until cool enough to handle.

Peel the potatoes, and pass them through a ricer or a food mill with a fine disc. Gently stir in the olive oil, and season them to taste with salt and pepper. Serve hot.

BRAISED SWISS CHARD AND CANNELLINI BEANS

Zimino di Bietole e Fagioli

This recipe hails from Maremma, in Tuscany, and a version of it was first featured in *Lidia's Italy*. Swiss chard is usually sold in a bunch tied around the stalks; look for young, tender bright-green leaves and thin stalks. In this recipe, cooked with cannellini beans, it can be a complete meal. A favorite in Tuscany and at our house, this dish is also delicious served with grilled meats. (I love grilled sausages with it.) It is good just off the stove, but it gets better when it rests a bit and is reheated. It will keep in the refrigerator for a few days, and also freezes very well.

SERVES 6

½ pound dried cannellini beans

1 teaspoon coarse sea salt or kosher salt, or to taste, plus ½ teaspoon for cooking dried beans

2 pounds big unblemished Swiss chard leaves

6 tablespoons extra-virgin olive oil, or more to taste

4 cloves garlic, peeled and thinly sliced

1 tablespoon tomato paste

½ teaspoon hot red pepper flakes, or to taste

1 cup canned Italian plum tomatoes (preferably San Marzano), crushed by hand

Rinse the beans, and put them in a bowl with cold water to cover by at least 4 inches. Let soak in a cool place for 8 hours or overnight. Drain the beans, and transfer them to a large saucepan with fresh cold water to cover by a few inches. Bring to a boil, partially covered, and cook the beans about 40 minutes, until tender but not mushy. Turn off the heat, and stir in ½ teaspoon salt; let the beans cool to absorb the cooking liquid and seasoning. Taste, and adjust the salt if needed.

Bring 6 quarts of water to the boil in a stockpot. Meanwhile, clean the Swiss chard leaves and cut off the stems and save them for a soup. Slice the leaves crosswise every 2 inches or so, into long strips. When the water is boiling, drop in all the sliced chard at once. Bring the water back to the boil, and cook the chard, covered, for about 15 minutes, until thoroughly tender—check a piece with a thick middle vein to be sure. Drain the cooked chard well in a colander. Drain the cannellini.

Heat ¼ cup of the olive oil and the sliced garlic in a large skillet over medium-high heat, stirring

(recipe continues)

frequently, until the garlic is sizzling, about 2 minutes. Drop the tomato paste into a clear spot in the pan, and stir and toast it for a minute. Toast the red pepper flakes in a cleared hot spot, too, then pour in the crushed tomatoes and stir everything together. Bring the tomatoes to a boil, and spill in the beans. Stir, season with salt, and bring back to simmer, stirring occasionally. Stir in the chard and bring to a boil over high heat. Cook rapidly for a couple of minutes to reduce the liquid, tossing the beans and greens over and over. As the juices thicken, drizzle the remaining 2 tablespoons olive oil all over, toss it in with the vegetables, and simmer for another 2 or 3 minutes, until most of the liquid has evaporated.

Serve right away, or set aside the skillet, covered, and reheat later.

BRUSSELS SPROUTS BRAISED WITH VINEGAR

Cavolini Brasati con Aceto

Brussels sprouts are not usually considered a favorite, but this recipe has converted many of my dinner guests into fans. People may shy away from them because of the intense cabbage flavor when they're cooked whole, but if you cut them in half and offset the flavor with some acidity (vinegar) everyone will love them.

SERVES 6

1½ pounds Brussels sprouts

¼ cup extra-virgin olive oil, plus more for drizzling over the finished dish

6 cloves garlic, peeled

Salt

1 cup water, or as needed

½ cup red wine vinegar

Freshly ground black pepper

Trim the core of the sprouts. Remove the discolored outer leaves, and cut each sprout vertically in half. Wash them thoroughly, and drain well.

Heat ¼ cup olive oil in a 3-quart braising pot or wide, deep skillet. Smash the garlic cloves with the side of a knife, and toss them into the oil, shaking the pan until they turn golden, about 2 minutes. Stir the sprouts into the oil, season them lightly with salt, and stir until they turn bright green, about 3 minutes. Pour in 1 cup water and the vinegar, and bring to a boil. Lower the heat so the liquid is simmering. Cook, uncovered, until the sprouts are tender and almost falling apart and the liquid is almost completely evaporated, 20 to 25 minutes. If the liquid is evaporated before the sprouts are tender, add more water, about ¼ cup at a time, as necessary. Season with salt and pepper to taste.

Spoon the sprouts into a warm serving bowl, drizzle with a little olive oil, and serve.

MARINATED WINTER SQUASH

Zucca Gialla Marinata

Squash is becoming ever more popular, and I love cooking with it and its fabulous flavor as well. This is a great side dish or appetizer—traditionally the *zucca* is fried before it is marinated, as I do here, but it is also delicious when grilled or boiled first. Though I recommend butternut squash, acorn, Hubbard, and other varieties will work as well.

SERVES 6 OR MORE AS AN APPETIZER
OR A SIDE DISH

1 cup apple cider vinegar or white vinegar

1 tablespoon sugar

½ teaspoon coarse sea salt or kosher salt, or more to taste

6 cloves garlic, peeled and sliced

1 tablespoon extra-virgin olive oil

2-pound butternut squash

1 cup vegetable oil, or as needed

10 to 20 fresh basil leaves, shredded

Mix the vinegar, sugar, and ¼ teaspoon salt together in a small saucepan. Let simmer over high heat until the marinade is reduced by half. Remove from the heat, drop in the garlic slices, and let the marinade cool. Stir in the olive oil.

Slice the squash in half lengthwise, and scrape out all the seeds. Peel the halves; with the cut side down, cut crosswise into ⅓-inch-thick half-rounds.

Pour a thin layer of vegetable oil into a deep skillet, and set over medium-high heat. When the oil sizzles on contact with the squash, fill the pan with a layer of slices, spaced slightly apart. Fry for about 3 minutes on the first side, then flip the slices over. Fry on the second side another 2 or 3 minutes, until the slices are cooked through (easy to pierce with the tines of a fork), crisped on the surface, and caramelized on the edges. Lift out the slices with a slotted spoon, draining off oil, and lay them on paper towels. Sprinkle some of the remaining salt lightly on the hot slices. Fry up all the squash, in batches, the same way.

Arrange a single layer of fried squash in the bottom of the marinating dish, and scatter some of the shredded basil leaves on top. Stir up the marinade, and drizzle a couple of spoonfuls over squash. Continue to layer the squash in the dish, topping each layer of fried slices with basil leaves and garlic marinade. All the seasonings should be used—drizzle any remaining marinade over the top layer of squash.

Wrap the dish in plastic, and marinate the squash for at least 3 hours and preferably overnight in the refrigerator; let it return to room temperature before serving.

EGGPLANT PARMIGIANA

Melanzane alla Parmigiana

This dish conjures up memories of Grandma's house in the minds of many, and part of those memories is the love that went into the cooking.

Frying the breaded eggplant is a traditional preparation, and it's become popular all over, as I discovered while researching *Lidia's Italy in America*. But you can make this recipe by just grilling the eggplant slices; it is not as flavorful, but it is much lighter and leaner. In Italy, this dish has always been served as a main dish; in America, it was for years considered a side, although now you find it often as a main dish here as well. An all-time favorite.

SERVES 6

3 medium eggplants, or 5 or 6 smaller eggplants (about 2½ to 3 pounds total)

1 tablespoon coarse sea or kosher salt

3 large eggs

1 teaspoon salt

All-purpose flour for dredging

2 cups plain breadcrumbs

½ cup vegetable oil, or as needed

½ cup olive oil, or as needed

4 cups Tomato Sauce (see page 103)

2 cups grated Grana Padano or Parmigiano-Reggiano cheese

12 fresh basil leaves

1 pound fresh mozzarella or Italian Fontina cheese, sliced ⅓ inch thick

Trim the stems and ends from the eggplants. Remove strips of peel about 1 inch wide from the eggplants, leaving about half the peel intact. Cut the eggplants lengthwise into ½-inch-thick slices, and place them in a colander. Sprinkle with the coarse salt, and let drain for 1 hour. Rinse the eggplant under cool running water, drain thoroughly, and pat dry.

Whisk the eggs and 1 teaspoon fine salt together in a baking pan or wide, shallow bowl. Spread the flour and breadcrumbs in an even layer in two separate wide, shallow bowls or on sheets of wax paper. Dredge the eggplant slices in flour, shaking off the excess. Dip the floured eggplant into the egg mixture, turning well to coat both sides evenly. Let excess egg drip back into the pan, then lay the eggplant in the bowl of breadcrumbs. Turn to coat both sides well with breadcrumbs, pressing with your hands until the breadcrumbs adhere.

Pour ½ cup each of the vegetable and olive oils into a medium skillet. Heat over medium-high heat until a corner of one of the eggplant slices gives

(recipe continues)

off a lively sizzle when dipped into the oil. Add as many of the eggplant slices as will fit without touching, and cook, turning once, until well browned on both sides, about 6 minutes. Remove the eggplant to a baking pan lined with paper towels, and repeat with the remaining eggplant slices. Adjust the heat as the eggplant cooks to prevent the bits of coating that fall off the eggplant slices from burning. Add oil to the pan during cooking, as necessary to keep the level the same.

Preheat the oven to 375 degrees F. Heat the tomato sauce to simmering, if cold or frozen, in a small saucepan over medium heat. Ladle enough sauce into a 9-by-13-inch baking dish to cover the bottom. Sprinkle with an even layer of grated cheese, and top with a layer of fried eggplant, pressing it down gently. Tear a few leaves of basil over the eggplant, and ladle about ¾ cup of the sauce to coat the top evenly. Sprinkle an even layer of grated cheese over the sauce and top with a layer of mozzarella or Fontina, using about one-third of the cheeses. Repeat the layering as described above two more times. Drizzle remaining sauce around the top and sprinkle with the remaining grated cheese. Cover the baking dish loosely with aluminum foil, and poke several holes in the foil with the tip of a knife. Bake for 30 minutes, until the cheese is bubbling.

Uncover, and continue baking until the top layer of cheese is golden, about 15 minutes. Let rest 10 to 20 minutes, then cut into squares and serve.

STUFFED TOMATOES

Pomodori Farciti al Forno

These stuffed tomatoes are best made in the summer, when tomatoes are abundant. Make sure the tomatoes are all approximately the same size and not overripe; firm tomatoes will yield good-looking results. This is a family favorite, and whether I make it as an appetizer or a side dish, there is never any left over. This dish is very good when hot out of the oven, but I prefer it at room temperature. It is a great buffet dish, or, when you are doing a lot of grilling, it can be your vegetable and starch all in one. For best results, make sure you fill the tomatoes loosely—do not overstuff, or they will be too dense after baking.

SERVES 8

1¼ teaspoons kosher salt

2 fresh bay leaves, or 3 dried

¾ cup Arborio rice

2 tablespoons extra-virgin olive oil

8 firm-ripe medium tomatoes

¾ cup fresh mozzarella cut into small cubes

2-ounce piece ham, cut in small cubes

½ cup plus 2 tablespoons grated Grana Padano or Parmigiano-Reggiano cheese

10 large basil leaves, chopped

½ teaspoon dried oregano

Preheat oven to 400 degrees F.

Prepare the rice: In a small pot, bring 2 cups water with ½ teaspoon salt to a boil with the bay leaves. Stir in the rice and 1 tablespoon of the olive oil. Bring to a simmer, and cook, uncovered, until rice is *al dente* and liquid is almost all gone, about 10 minutes. Scrape into a bowl to cool.

Slice the tops off the tomatoes, reserving for later. Scoop out the inner flesh of the tomatoes with a spoon, leaving a thick shell. As you work, put the flesh in a strainer set over a bowl to collect the juices. Once all of the tomatoes are scooped out, season the insides of the tomatoes with ½ teaspoon of the salt.

Chop the tomato flesh, and put it in the bowl with the rice. Add the mozzarella, ham, ½ cup of the grated cheese, the basil, the oregano, and the remaining ¼ teaspoon salt. Toss to combine.

Pour the reserved tomato juices into the bottom of a large baking dish. Evenly divide the stuffing between the tomatoes. Arrange the cut-off tomato tops in the baking dish, cut side down, and place a stuffed tomato on each top. Depending on the size of your tomatoes, you may have a little leftover stuffing. If so, roll it into "meatballs" and place in the spaces between tomatoes in the baking dish. Drizzle tomatoes with the remaining tablespoon of olive oil, and sprinkle tops with the remaining grated cheese. Bake until the tomatoes are soft and juicy and the stuffing is browned on top, about 20 to 25 minutes.

SEAFOOD

SHRIMP PREPARED IN THE SCAMPI STYLE

Scampi

Everybody seems to like crunchy, garlicky shrimp. The one cardinal mistake with shrimp is to overcook them. Using this method, where one makes the flavored butter first, the chance of over-cooking the shrimp is minimized, and the results are delicious.

SERVES 6

2 tablespoons extra-virgin olive oil

3 large cloves garlic, peeled and minced

2 tablespoons finely chopped shallots

Salt and freshly ground black pepper to taste

½ cup dry white wine

2 tablespoons freshly squeezed lemon juice

8 tablespoons unsalted butter, at room temperature

2 teaspoons minced fresh parsley

2 teaspoons minced fresh tarragon

36 medium to large shrimp (about 3½ pounds)

6 to 8 sprigs fresh thyme

To make the flavored butter: Heat the olive oil in a small skillet over medium heat. Add the garlic, and cook until pale golden, about 1 minute. Stir in the shallots, season generously with salt and pepper, and continue cooking, shaking the skillet, until the shallots are wilted, about 2 minutes. Add ¼ cup of the wine, bring to a boil, and cook until about half of the wine has evaporated. Stir in 1 tablespoon of the lemon juice, and boil until almost all of the liquid has evaporated. Transfer to a small bowl, and cool completely. Add the butter, parsley, and tarragon, and beat until blended. To make the butter easier to handle, spoon it onto plastic wrap and roll it into a log shape, completely wrapped in plastic. Chill thoroughly. (The flavored butter can be made several hours or up to a few days in advance.)

Place the rack in the lowest position in the oven and preheat oven to 475 degrees F. Peel the shrimp, leaving the tail and last shell segment attached. De-vein the shrimp by making a shallow cut along the curved back of the shrimp and extracting the black or gray vein that runs the length of the shrimp. Split the body of the shrimp half open with a paring knife, leaving the tail part whole.

Using some of the flavored butter, lightly grease a low-sided baking pan, such as a jelly-roll pan, or an ovenproof sauté pan into which the shrimp fit comfortably without touching. Place each shrimp on the work surface with the underside of the tail facing away from you. With your fingers, roll each slit part of the shrimp underneath each side of the shrimp, lifting the tail up.

Set the prepped shrimp, tails up, on the buttered pan as you work, leaving some space between each shrimp. Cut the remaining flavored butter into ½-inch cubes, and disperse the cubes among the shrimp. Add the remaining wine and lemon juice. Scatter the thyme sprigs over and around the shrimp. Season with salt and pepper, and place the pan on the oven rack. Bake until the shrimp are firm and crunchy and barely opaque in the center, about 5 minutes. Transfer the shrimp to a hot platter, or divide among warm plates.

Bring the remaining juices in the pan to a boil over high heat on top of the stove until the sauce is lightly thickened, 1 to 2 minutes. Spoon the sauce over the shrimp as is, or strain it first for a more velvety texture. Serve immediately.

GRILLED CALAMARI

Calamari alla Griglia

The primary ingredient in any fish preparation must be super-fresh fish. Nowhere is that more evident than in grilling calamari. This dish can be prepared on a charcoal grill or in a cast-iron pan or griddle, but in either case, the temperature should be good and hot, so the calamari cook very quickly. For easy handling, thread the calamari bodies onto a skewer—one or two per skewer, depending on the size. (Thread the tentacles onto a separate skewer, without crowding them, since they will need a few additional minutes to cook.)

SERVES 6

8 medium squid (about 3 pounds), cleaned, leaving skin on

¼ cup extra-virgin olive oil, plus more for drizzling over the cooked squid if you like

6 cloves garlic, peeled and sliced

1 tablespoon fresh thyme leaves

½ teaspoon salt

½ teaspoon hot red pepper flakes

Chopped fresh Italian parsley

Toss the cleaned calamari bodies and tentacles together with the olive oil, garlic, thyme, salt, and red pepper in a bowl, until the calamari is coated. Cover the bowl, and marinate in refrigerator for 1 hour, or up to overnight.

Prepare a charcoal grill well ahead, so it is hot, or heat a wide cast-iron skillet or griddle over high heat until a drop of water bounces and sizzles. Lay the squid on the grill or in the skillet. Set a heavy skillet on top of the calamari to weight it down so as much of the calamari as possible makes contact with the hot grill or skillet. (This makes it easier for the calamari to cook evenly and brown well.) Cook until golden on one side, about 4 minutes, then flip and cook 3 minutes on the other side.

Transfer to a warm platter, and drizzle with additional extra-virgin olive oil if you like. Sprinkle with chopped Italian parsley, and serve immediately.

SOLE MEUNIÈRE

Filetto di Sogliola al Limone

This light fish in a lemony sauce, which always appears on Italian and French menus, has remained a favorite for decades. I served it in my first restaurant, and continue to serve it today. I recommend using fillet of sole in this recipe, but the fillet of any fish prepared this way is delicious. It is easy to prepare, and even kids love it. The result is a puckery lemon finish, with briny capers.

You know how much I love olive oil, but there is a time and place for everything. When sautéing foods that cook quickly, like these sole fillets, using some butter along with the oil helps the sole brown before they overcook. Thicker sole or flounder fillets are ideal for this dish, but if yours are thinner, you may find it easier to handle them if you cut them in half first. Traditionally the fillets are simmered in the sauce, but I like to cook the sauce separately and spoon it around the sole fillets—they stay crispier that way.

SERVES 4

5 tablespoons extra-virgin olive oil, plus more for finishing the sauce if you like

6 tablespoons unsalted butter

6 fillets gray or lemon sole, approximately 2½ pounds

All-purpose flour for dredging

5 cloves garlic, crushed and peeled

12 thin lemon slices (about 2 lemons)

3 tablespoons drained tiny capers

¼ cup freshly squeezed lemon juice

¼ cup dry white wine

½ cup vegetable stock or water

2 tablespoons chopped fresh parsley

Salt and freshly ground black pepper

Preheat the oven to 250 degrees F. Heat 3 tablespoons of the olive oil and 4 tablespoons of the butter in a large, heavy skillet over medium-high heat until the butter is foaming.

Dredge the fillets in the flour to coat both sides lightly. Gently lay as many of the fillets in the pan as fit without touching. Cook just until the underside is lightly browned, about 4 minutes. Flip them gently with a wide metal spatula, and cook until the second side is browned and the fish is opaque in the center, about 2 minutes. Transfer them with the spatula to a baking sheet, and keep them warm in the oven. Repeat if necessary with the remaining fillets, adjusting the heat under the skillet to prevent the bits of flour in the pan from burning.

When all the sole fillets have been browned, carefully wipe out the skillet with a wad of paper towels. Add the remaining olive oil and the remaining butter and crushed garlic, and return to medium

(recipe continues)

heat. When the butter is foaming, slide in the lemon slices, and cook, stirring gently, until they are sizzling and lightly browned. Stir in the capers, and heat until they are sizzling, about 1 minute. Pour in the lemon juice and wine, bring to a boil, and cook until reduced by about half. Pour in the vegetable stock, bring to a boil, and boil until the sauce is lightly thickened, about 2 minutes. If you like, drizzle in a tablespoon or two of olive oil to enrich the sauce. Sprinkle in the parsley, and taste, seasoning with salt and pepper if you like.

Remove the sole from the oven, and set one fillet in the center of each plate. Fish the lemon slices out of the sauce, and top each fillet with two of them. Spoon the sauce around the fillets, dividing it evenly. Serve immediately.

SAVORY SEAFOOD STEW

Zuppa di Pesce

The *zuppa di pesce* that you are most likely familiar with was based on garlic and tomato sauce, which was simmered along with assorted fish to make a savory, chunky dish. This version is more in a *brodetto* style (my favorite—lighter and clearer). This kind of preparation can be found with slight variations along the entire northern coast of Italy.

SERVES 6

2 quarts water

One 35-ounce can Italian plum tomatoes (preferably San Marzano), with their liquid

1½ cups dry white wine

4 small leeks, white parts only, trimmed and cleaned; 2 cut into 3-inch lengths (about 2 cups), 2 sliced ½ inch thick (about 2 cups)

2 medium carrots, trimmed and sliced thick

2 large onions, 1 cut into thick slices, 1 thinly sliced

10 sprigs fresh thyme

Zest of ½ lemon, removed in wide strips with a vegetable peeler

½ cup extra-virgin olive oil

Salt

8 cloves garlic, peeled

4 medium calamari (about 1¼ pounds), cleaned, tentacles left whole, bodies cut crosswise into ½-inch rings

10 medium sea scallops (about ½ pound)

8 ounces fresh, firm-textured fish fillets, such as salmon, snapper, or swordfish, skin removed, cut into 1-inch pieces

2 cups cooked cannellini beans (canned is okay) (optional)

24 mussels, preferably cultivated, cleaned

12 jumbo shrimp, peeled and deveined (about ½ pound)

¼ cup chopped fresh Italian parsley

Freshly ground black pepper to taste

Garlic Bread (see page 20) or crusty Italian bread

Make the soup base: Combine the water, tomatoes, wine, 3-inch leeks, carrots, thickly sliced onion, thyme, and lemon zest in a saucepan, and bring to a boil. Lower the heat to keep at a lively simmer, and cook until reduced by about one-third, about 45 minutes. Stir in ¼ cup olive oil, season the mixture lightly with salt, and continue to simmer until the liquid portion of the soup base is reduced to about 8 cups, about 20 minutes. Strain the soup base into a 3-quart saucepan, and keep it warm over low heat. Discard the solids. (The soup base may be prepared up to 3 days in advance and refrigerated.)

If you have prepared the soup base in advance, bring it to a simmer in a medium saucepan. Adjust the heat to very low and keep it warm. Heat the

(recipe continues)

remaining ¼ cup olive oil in a large (about 8-quart) heavy pot over medium heat. Add the thinly sliced onion, ½-inch-sliced leeks, and garlic, and cook, stirring, until the onion is wilted but still crunchy, about 4 minutes. Add the calamari, and cook, stirring, until they turn opaque, about 2 minutes. Pour in all but 1 cup of the soup base, and bring to a boil. Stir in the scallops, fish fillets, and beans (if using). Adjust the heat to maintain a simmer, and cook until the seafood is barely opaque at the center, about 5 minutes.

Meanwhile, add the mussels to the soup base remaining in the saucepan. Increase the heat to high, cover the saucepan, and steam over medium heat, shaking the pan occasionally, until the mussels open, about 3 minutes.

Stir the shrimp, parsley, and steamed mussels in their shells into the large pot of soup. Simmer until the shrimp are cooked through, about 1 minute. Check the seasoning, adding salt, if necessary, and pepper. Ladle into warm soup bowls, passing a basket of the bread of your choice separately.

SHRIMP BUZARA STYLE

Gamberoni alla Buzara

Everyone loves shrimp, and how better to savor them than in this tasty sauce, one of my childhood favorites? This recipe is a traditional Istrian recipe for a species of shrimp similar to langoustines, not found in American waters, and it comes from the area around Trieste, Istria, and Dalmatia, where some of the best scampi are caught. Here I give you the recipe and technique of *langoustine alla buzara* so you can prepare this delicious dish with shrimp for your family and guests.

SERVES 4 TO 6

2 pounds super colossal shrimp (10 to 12 per pound)

1 tablespoon tomato paste

1 cup hot light fish stock

¼ cup olive oil

½ cup finely chopped onion

2 cloves garlic, crushed and peeled

Salt and freshly ground black pepper to taste

1 cup dry white wine

1 tablespoon breadcrumbs

1 tablespoon chopped fresh Italian parsley

Using poultry shears or a sharp paring knife, cut through the outer curve of the shrimp shells from end to end, but don't remove the shells. Rinse the shrimp under cold running water, and devein.

Dissolve the tomato paste in the hot stock. Heat 2 tablespoons of olive oil in a medium saucepan. Add the onion and garlic, and sauté over moderately high heat until golden. Season with salt and pepper, add the wine, and bring to a boil. Add the stock-and-tomato-paste mixture, reduce the heat, and simmer 20 minutes.

Meantime, heat the remaining oil in a large skillet, add the shrimp, and sauté (in two batches) 1 minute on each side. Drain off the oil, return all the shrimp to the skillet, and add the sauce. Cover, and cook over high heat, stirring occasionally, until the shrimp are just cooked through, about 2 or 3 minutes. Sprinkle with breadcrumbs and parsley, mix well, and cook a minute longer, uncovered. Serve immediately.

LOBSTER IN ZESTY TOMATO SAUCE

Aragosta in Brodetto

This is how my grandma cooked lobster when we were lucky enough that my fisherman uncle Emilio had caught one or two. Lobster cooked slowly with tomato, vinegar, and onion is delicious on its own, but we served it over polenta, or to dress pasta. Using vinegar in this recipe is an old technique of Venetian sailors to preserve their food while at sea—it actually gives a nice balance to the sweetness of the lobster. Needless to say, it is one of my favorite ways to eat lobster.

SERVES 6

Six 1¼-pound Maine lobsters

½ teaspoon salt, plus more for pasta (optional)

⅓ cup vegetable oil

1 cup all-purpose flour for dredging

½ cup extra-virgin olive oil

1½ cups diced onion

1 cup diced scallions

6 tablespoons tomato paste

½ cup red wine vinegar

3 cups hot water

4 cups canned Italian plum tomatoes (preferably San Marzano), crushed

Hot red pepper flakes

½ cup chopped fresh Italian parsley leaves

1 pound spaghetti (optional)

Cut the live lobsters into serving pieces according to the directions for the Lobster Fra Diavolo (see page 64). If you plan to serve the lobster with pasta, bring 4 quarts salted water to a boil.

Heat the vegetable oil in a large skillet over medium-high heat. Meanwhile, lightly coat the exposed meat of the lobster tails with flour, shaking off excess flour. The oil is hot enough when a corner of a lobster tail dipped in it gives off a lively sizzle. Add lobster tails, meat side down, and cook, shaking the skillet occasionally, until golden brown, about 2 minutes. Remove the tails from the oil, and set them aside.

Heat ⅓ cup of the olive oil in a large, wide saucepan over medium heat. Add the onion and scallions, and cook until translucent, 3 to 4 minutes. Add the lobster body pieces, and cook, stirring, until they turn bright red, about 5 minutes. Stir in tomato paste, and cook for 5 minutes. Blend the vinegar with the hot water, then pour it into the pan and bring to a full boil. Add the tomatoes and salt, bring to a boil, and cook 3 minutes. Stir in red pepper flakes to taste.

Remove the lobster bodies with tongs, allowing all juices to drain back into sauce, and keep them warm; they may be served on a communal platter in the center of the table. The most delicate meat is in those bodies and should not be wasted.

Add the claws to the pan, and cook 7 minutes. Add the reserved tails, the lobster legs, the parsley, and the remaining olive oil. Simmer until the lobster tails are fully cooked, 3 to 5 minutes longer over high heat, skimming off all surface foam. Remove the tails and claws, and keep them warm under aluminum foil. Bring the sauce to a boil, and cook until slightly thickened. Arrange the lobster pieces on a warm platter, and spoon the hot sauce over them.

To serve the brodetto with pasta, cook and drain the pasta and return it to the pot. Add half the lobster sauce, and toss to coat over low heat. Transfer the pasta to a platter, and flank with the lobster pieces. Spoon the remaining sauce over the lobster.

POULTRY AND MEATS

LAMB STEW WITH OLIVES

Agnello 'ncip 'nciape

This is one of those delicious dishes that are complex in taste but easy to prepare. Many home cooks are intimidated by lamb, but my readers tell me that they find this recipe both tasty and easy. Boneless lamb is readily available, and boneless lamb shoulder or leg meat is just fine for this dish.

SERVES 6 OR MORE

3½ pounds boneless lamb shoulder or leg

2 teaspoons kosher salt

¼ cup extra-virgin olive oil

7 plump cloves garlic, crushed and peeled

½ teaspoon hot red pepper flakes, or to taste

2 tablespoons fresh rosemary leaves, stripped from the branch

1 cup white wine

2 tablespoons red-wine vinegar

1½ cups brine-cured green Italian olives or oil-cured black Italian olives, crushed and pitted

Trim the exterior fat from the lamb shoulder or leg, and cut the meat into 2-inch pieces, removing fat and bits of cartilage as you find them. Pat the pieces dry with paper towels, and season all over with half the salt.

Pour the olive oil into a Dutch oven, and set it over medium heat. Scatter in the crushed garlic cloves and red pepper flakes. When the garlic is sizzling, lay in all the lamb pieces in one layer, scatter the rosemary on top, and season with the remaining salt. When the meat starts to sizzle, cover the pan, lower the heat, and let cook gently, browning slowly and releasing its fat and juices, about 10 minutes. Uncover the pan, turn the pieces, and move them around the pan to cook evenly; then cover, and cook for another 10 minutes. Turn again, and continue cooking, covered, for another 10 to 15 minutes, until the lamb is nicely browned all over and the pan juices have thickened and caramelized. (If there is a lot of fat in the bottom of the pan, tilt the skillet and spoon off the fat from one side.)

Stir the wine and vinegar together, and pour them into the skillet, swirling them with the pan juices. Bring the liquids to a boil, and cook them down quickly to form a syrupy sauce. Drop the olives into the pan, all around the lamb chunks, then cover, and adjust the heat so the liquid maintains a bubbling simmer. Cook for another 10 minutes or so, which will concentrate the juices and marry the flavors. Cook uncovered for a few final minutes, tumbling the meat and olives in the pan, coating them with the sauce.

Serve right from the skillet, or heap the meat chunks on a platter or in a shallow serving bowl. Spoon out any sauce and olives left in the pan, and drizzle over the lamb.

SAUSAGE AND PEPPERS

Salsiccia con Peperoni

The key to making really wonderful sausage and peppers is to caramelize each ingredient separately—sausages, peppers, and onions—then to pile them into a baking dish and finish them in the oven. This way, all the sweet juices remain in the sausages and vegetables. Sausage and peppers is an all-time favorite, found at every Italian festivity, carnival, and street fair in America and at most large Italian American family gatherings, as featured in *Lidia's Italian-American Kitchen*.

SERVES 8 (INGREDIENTS CAN EASILY
BE HALVED TO SERVE 4)

1 pound white, shiitake, or crimini mushrooms (or a mix of two or three kinds)

16 links sweet Italian sausages, with or without fennel seeds (about 3 pounds)

¼ cup extra-virgin olive oil, or as needed

8 cloves garlic, peeled

3 large yellow onions, cut into 1-inch wedges (about 5 cups)

6 pickled cherry peppers, stemmed and seeded but left whole

2 medium yellow and 2 medium red bell peppers, cored and seeded, cut into 1-inch strips (about 6 cups total)

Prepare the mushrooms: Trim the stems from the shiitakes, if using. Trim the stems from the white and crimini mushrooms if you like. Cut any mushrooms with caps larger than 2 inches in half; leave smaller mushrooms whole.

Poke the sausages all over with a fork. Divide ¼ cup olive oil between two large, heavy skillets, and heat them over medium heat. Divide the sausages between the skillets, and cook, turning occasionally, until the sausages are well browned on all sides. In the meantime whack the garlic with the flat side of a knife and toss half the cloves into each skillet. Transfer the browned sausages and garlic to a baking dish, leaving the fat behind.

Preheat the oven to 400 degrees F.

Scatter the onions and cherry peppers over the fat in one of the skillets, and the mushrooms over the fat in the other. Cook, stirring often, until the onions are browned and wilted but still quite crunchy, about 8 minutes. Cook the mushrooms until they have absorbed the fat in the skillet and have begun to brown, about 6 minutes.

Slide the mushrooms into the baking dish. Spoon the onions into the baking dish, leaving behind some of the fat in the skillet. (If there is not enough fat left to coat the bottom of the skillet, pour in enough olive oil to do so.) Add the bell peppers to the skillet, and cook, tossing frequently, just until wilted but still quite crunchy, about 6 minutes. Slide the peppers into the baking dish, toss all the ingredients together well, and place in the oven.

Bake, uncovered, tossing occasionally, until the vegetables are tender but still firm and no trace of pink remains in the sausages, about 25 minutes. Serve hot.

SAUSAGES WITH FENNEL AND OLIVES

Salsicce con Finocchio e Olive

I love fennel with good Italian sausage for a main course, a sandwich, or even to dress pasta; this combination works. Here meat and vegetables are skillet-cooked, first separately and then together, and their flavors merge and concentrate. It may seem that a lot of fennel is called for, but in cooking, fennel reduces down, caramelizing as it cooks. Fennel prepared this way is excellent with any grilled meats, even with grilled fish. I am glad to say that the American palate is slowly discovering fennel, and this recipe provides an easy, tasty way to enjoy it.

SERVES 6

4 tablespoons extra-virgin olive oil

12 sweet Italian sausages (about 2 pounds)

1 cup dry white wine

6 plump cloves garlic, crushed and peeled

¼ teaspoon hot red pepper flakes, or to taste

1 cup large green olives, squashed to open them to remove pits

3½ pounds fresh fennel bulbs, trimmed and cut into 1-inch chunks (see page 69 for technique)

½ teaspoon salt

Pour half the olive oil into a big skillet over medium-high heat. Lay in all the sausages; cook them for 5 minutes or more, rolling them over occasionally, until they're nicely browned on all sides. Pour in the wine, and boil it until it is reduced by half. Remove the sausages to a platter, and pour over them the wine remaining in the pan.

Add the remaining olive oil to the skillet, toss in the garlic cloves, and cook for a minute, until sizzling. Clear a hot spot, and cook the red pepper flakes in it for a few seconds, then scatter the crushed olives in the pan; toss and cook for a couple of minutes.

Add the fennel chunks to the pan, and stir. Season the vegetables with ½ teaspoon salt, cover the skillet, and cook over medium-high heat for 20 minutes, stirring now and then, until the fennel softens, and begins to color. Add a bit of water to the pan if the fennel remains hard; you want it to be wilted but not mushy.

When the fennel is cooked through, return the sausages and wine to the skillet. Turn and tumble the meat and vegetables together, and cook, uncovered, another 5 minutes. Adjust the seasoning to taste; serve piping hot.

CHICKEN IN BEER

Pollo alla Birra

Every household has its favorite rendition of roasted chicken, and a simple, perfectly roasted chicken is the best. But why not diversify now and then? At our house we often give it a twist and roast the chicken in beer with clove and cinnamon, as they do in Trentino–Alto Adige, a region of northern Italy featured in *Lidia Cooks from the Heart of Italy.* The beer gives it a complexity of flavors, and leaves the chicken moist with a great glossy skin. Not only do you have the beer-flavored roasted chicken in this recipe, but the vegetables roasted along with the chicken are also a great side dish.

SERVES 6

A 3½-to-4-pound roasting chicken

2 teaspoons kosher salt

2 medium onions, peeled and quartered

1 large carrot, peeled, halved crosswise, and quartered lengthwise (about 4 ounces)

2 medium parsnips, peeled, halved crosswise, and quartered lengthwise (about 6 ounces total)

2 tablespoons fresh sage leaves

4 whole cloves

1 cinnamon stick

1½ cups light stock (chicken, turkey, or vegetable broth) or water

1½ cups (one 12-ounce bottle) flavorful beer or ale

1 cup nonalcoholic apple cider, preferably unfiltered

Arrange a rack in the middle of the oven, and heat to 400 degrees F. Trim the excess fat from the chicken, and season it inside and out with half of the salt.

Scatter the onions, carrot, parsnips, sage, cloves, and cinnamon in the pot, sprinkle over this the rest of the salt, and set the chicken on top of the vegetables. Put the pot on the stove, pour in the stock, beer, and apple cider, and bring to a simmer over medium heat. Cook, uncovered, for about 15 minutes on top of the stove.

Put the pot in the oven, and roast the chicken for about 30 minutes, basting with the pan juices two or three times. Cover the chicken with a sheet of aluminum foil to prevent overbrowning, and roast another 30 minutes. Remove the foil, and roast another 20 to 30 minutes, basting frequently, until the chicken and vegetables are cooked through and tender.

Remove the chicken to a warm platter, and surround with the vegetables. Bring the pan juices to a boil on top of the stove, and cook until reduced by half. Carve the chicken at the table, and spoon some of the pan juices on top.

CHICKEN CACCIATORE

Pollo alla Cacciatore

Chicken cacciatore has been prepared in Italian homes forever, and it is usually made by cutting up a whole chicken. But if you don't want to cut up a whole chicken, you can buy pieces—get all legs and thighs, which is what I like. Best of all, though, is to make this dish with an organic older hen. If you do make this with an older hen, increase the cooking time by 20 minutes, adding more water or stock as needed to keep the hen covered while it cooks.

SERVES 6

2 broiler chickens (about 2½ pounds each, preferably free-range)

Salt and freshly ground black pepper to taste

All-purpose flour for dredging

¼ cup vegetable oil

¼ cup extra-virgin olive oil

1 small yellow onion, cut into 1-inch cubes (about 1 cup)

½ cup dry white wine

One 28-ounce can Italian plum tomatoes (preferably San Marzano), with liquid, crushed

1 teaspoon dried oregano, preferably the Sicilian or Greek type dried on the branch, crumbled

2 cups sliced white or shiitake mushrooms (about 8 ounces)

1 red and 1 yellow bell pepper, cored and seeded, cut into ½-inch strips (about 2 cups total)

Cut each chicken into twelve pieces: With a sturdy knife or kitchen shears, remove the backbone by cutting along both sides. Remove the wing tips. (You can save the backbone, wing tips, and giblets—except for the liver—to make chicken stock another time. Or, if you like, cut the backbone in half crosswise and add it to this dish.) Place the chicken, breast side down, on a cutting board, and cut it into halves by cutting through the breastbone lengthwise. Cut off the wing at the joint that connects it to the breast, then cut each wing in half at the joint. Separate the leg from the breast. Cut the leg in half at the joint. Cut the breast in half crosswise, giving the knife a good whack when you get to the bone to separate the breast cleanly into halves. Repeat with the remaining chicken.

Season the chicken pieces generously with salt and pepper. Dredge the pieces in flour, coating them lightly and tapping off excess flour. Heat the vegetable oil in a wide braising pan with 2 tablespoons of the olive oil until a piece of chicken dipped in the oil gives off a very lively sizzle. Add as many pieces of chicken to the pan as will fit without touching (do not crowd the chicken; you can always brown it in batches). Remove the chicken pieces from the skillet as they brown, adding some of the remaining pieces of chicken to take their place. After browning all the chicken and removing it from the skillet, add the onion to the fat remaining in the pan and cook, stirring, for 5 minutes.

Pour the wine into the pan, bring to a boil, and cook until reduced by half, about 3 minutes. Add the tomatoes and oregano, season lightly with salt and pepper, and bring to a boil. Tuck the chicken into the sauce, adjust the heat to a gentle boil, and cover the pan. Cook, stirring a few times, for 20 minutes.

Meanwhile, heat the remaining 2 tablespoons olive oil in a large skillet over medium-high heat. Add the mushrooms and peppers, and toss until the peppers are wilted but still quite crunchy, about 8 minutes. Season the vegetables with salt.

Add the peppers and mushrooms to the chicken pan. Cook, covered, until the chicken and vegetables are tender, 10 to 15 minutes. (Check the level of the liquid as it cooks; there should be enough liquid to barely cover the chicken. If necessary, add small amounts of water to maintain the level of liquid as the chicken cooks.) Serve the chicken pieces nestled between the vegetables on a platter.

CHICKEN PARMIGIANA, NEW STYLE

Pollo alla Parmigiana

Chicken parmigiana is all-time favorite among Italian Americans, and my grandchildren are no exception. But this is a more contemporary version of the classic. Instead of coating a thin, breaded, and fried chicken cutlet with tomato sauce, I like to top the chicken with slices of fresh tomatoes and slices of fresh mozzarella or Fontina cheese. I use a light tomato sauce made with fresh tomatoes and basil to finish the plate.

SERVES 4

4 boneless, skinless chicken thighs or breasts (about 1½ pounds)

Salt and freshly ground black pepper to taste

All-purpose flour for dredging

¾ cup fine dry plain breadcrumbs

2 large eggs

1 cup vegetable oil, or as needed

3 ripe plum tomatoes, cored and thinly sliced

6 ounces fresh mozzarella or Italian Fontina cheese, sliced thin

FOR THE SAUCE

¼ cup extra-virgin olive oil, plus more for drizzling over the finished dish

6 cloves garlic, peeled

8 ripe tomatoes, or 12 ripe plum tomatoes, peeled, seeded, and chopped

¼ cup shredded fresh basil leaves

Cut off any fat, bone, and gristle remaining on the chicken thighs. Place two thighs between two sheets of plastic wrap. Pound them lightly with the toothed side of a meat mallet to a more or less even thickness.

Season the chicken thighs lightly with salt and pepper. Spread out the flour and breadcrumbs on two separate plates. Beat the eggs in a wide, shallow bowl until thoroughly blended. Dredge the chicken in flour to coat lightly, and tap off excess flour. Dip the floured thighs in the beaten egg, and hold them over the bowl to let the excess egg drip back into the bowl. Transfer the chicken, one piece at a time, to the plate of breadcrumbs; turn it to coat with breadcrumbs, patting gently and making sure that each thigh is well coated.

Heat the vegetable oil in a wide, heavy skillet over medium-high heat until a corner of one of the coated thighs gives off a lively sizzle when dipped in the oil. Add to the oil as many of the chicken pieces as fit without touching. Fry, turning once, until golden on both sides and cooked through, about 8 minutes. Remove to a baking sheet lined with paper towels, and drain well.

(recipe continues)

Remove the paper towels from the baking sheet. Top each chicken thigh with overlapping slices of tomato, dividing the tomatoes evenly. Drape the sliced cheese over the tomatoes to cover the chicken completely.

Preheat the oven to 400 degrees F.

Prepare the sauce: Heat 3 tablespoons of the olive oil in a wide nonreactive skillet. Whack the garlic cloves with the side of a knife, and drop them into the oil. Cook, shaking the pan, until golden brown, about 2 minutes. Carefully slide the chopped tomatoes into the skillet, season lightly with salt and pepper, and cook until lightly thickened, about 10 minutes. Remove from the heat, and set aside.

Bake the chicken until the cheese is lightly browned, about 10 minutes. While the chicken is baking, reheat the tomato sauce to keep it simmering, stir in the basil, and taste, seasoning with salt and pepper if necessary. Spoon the sauce onto a heated platter or plates, and place the baked chicken over the sauce. Drizzle the remaining olive oil over the sauce, and serve immediately.

CHICKEN BREAST WITH EGGPLANT AND FONTINA CHEESE

Pollo alla Sorrentina

The name of this dish, "alla Sorrentina," means it originated in Sorrento, across the bay from Naples, and whenever you see "alla Sorrentina" it is a good indicator that the dish will contain eggplant and melted cheese—although I have sometimes substituted zucchini, asparagus, and squash for eggplant, according to the season. In my research throughout the United States for *Lidia's Italy in America*, this recipe appeared on the tables of many Italian American restaurants and homes in slightly different versions.

SERVES 6

1 medium eggplant (about 1¼ pounds)

Salt

6 tablespoons extra-virgin olive oil

Six 6-ounce boneless, skinless chicken breasts

Freshly ground black pepper

6 slices (about 3 ounces) imported Italian prosciutto, cut in half

5 tablespoons unsalted butter

All-purpose flour for dredging

6 cloves garlic, peeled

½ cup dry white wine

About 1 cup hot chicken stock or canned low-sodium chicken broth

¼ cup canned Italian plum tomatoes (preferably San Marzano), seeded and chopped

12 fresh basil leaves, plus more (optional) for decorating the plates

6 ounces Italian Fontina cheese, cut into thin slices

2 tablespoons Tomato Sauce (see page 103) or liquid from the canned tomatoes

Trim the stem from the eggplant. Remove strips of peel about 1 inch wide, leaving about half the peel intact, and cut the eggplant into 1-inch crosswise slices. Sprinkle a baking sheet with salt, arrange the slices over the salt, and sprinkle with more salt. Let them stand until both sides are wet, about 30 minutes. Rinse the eggplant under cool running water, drain thoroughly, and pat dry.

Preheat the oven to 400 degrees F. Wipe the baking sheet clean, and oil it generously, using about half the oil. Arrange the eggplant on the baking sheet, and turn to coat the slices with oil. Roast until tender and well browned, turning them and rotating them in the pan as necessary, about 20 minutes. Remove and cool. Increase the oven temperature to 450 degrees F.

Cut each chicken breast in half on a bias, and lightly pound it. Season the chicken very lightly with salt and pepper (the prosciutto will give the dish plenty of salt as is), and layer each piece of chicken with half a slice of the prosciutto, tapping the pro-

(recipe continues)

sciutto with the back of a knife so it adheres to the meat.

Heat 2 tablespoons of the remaining olive oil and 2 tablespoons of the butter in a heavy, wide skillet over medium heat. Dredge the chicken in flour to coat both sides lightly, tapping off excess flour, and add as many to the skillet, prosciutto side down, as will fit without overlapping. Cook just until the prosciutto is light golden, about 2 minutes. Turn, and cook until the second side is browned, about 2 minutes. Remove, and drain on paper towels. Repeat with the remaining chicken, adding more oil if necessary.

After removing the last piece of chicken from the skillet, pour in the remaining oil, and scatter the garlic in the skillet. Cook, turning, until golden brown, about 3 minutes. (Lower the heat, if necessary, so the bits of flour that stick to the pan don't burn while the garlic is browning.) Pour the wine into the skillet, bring to a boil, and boil until it's almost completely evaporated. Pour in the stock, and drop in the remaining 3 tablespoons butter. Bring to a boil, stir in the chopped tomatoes, and boil until the sauce is lightly reduced and glossy, about 4 minutes.

Meanwhile, arrange the scaloppine side by side in a baking dish. Cover them with the eggplant, cutting or tearing the slices as necessary to cover all the scaloppine more or less evenly, and top each with a leaf of basil. Divide the Fontina slices evenly over the eggplant, dotting each Fontina slice with a dab of tomato sauce. Pour the pan sauce around the chicken, and bake until the cheese is melted and lightly browned in places and the sauce is lightly thickened, about 10 minutes. Transfer the bubbly chicken to serving plates, placing two on each. Spoon the sauce—through a strainer if you like—around the plates. Decorate the plates with additional basil leaves if desired.

MY MOTHER'S CHICKEN AND POTATOES

Pollo e Patate della Mamma

Chicken and potatoes, cooked together in a big cast-iron skillet until the chicken is crisp and moist at the same time, is my mother's specialty. Growing up, my brother and I demanded it every week; a generation later, our kids, Tanya and Joe, and my brother Franco's children, Eric, Paul, and Estelle, clamored for it, too. And now the next generation of little ones are asking their great-grandmother to make chicken and potatoes for them. This is by far one of our most requested recipes; I am sure Grandma's personality must have something to do with it, but the tasty dish has merits all its own.

SERVES 4

FOR THE BASIC CHICKEN AND POTATOES

2½ pounds chicken legs or assorted pieces (bone-in)

½ cup canola oil

½ teaspoon salt, or more to taste

1 pound Red Bliss potatoes, preferably no bigger than 2 inches across

2 tablespoons extra-virgin olive oil, or more as needed

2 medium-small onions, peeled and quartered lengthwise

2 short branches fresh rosemary with plenty of needles

FOR MY SPECIAL TOUCHES — TRY EITHER OR BOTH

4 to 6 ounces sliced bacon (5 or 6 slices)

1 or 2 pickled cherry peppers, sweet or hot—or more!—cut in half and seeded

Rinse the chicken pieces, and pat dry with paper towels. Trim off excess skin and all visible fat. Cut the drumsticks from the thighs. If using breast halves, cut each into two small pieces.

Make the bacon roll-ups: Cut the bacon slices in half crosswise, and roll each strip into a neat, tight cylinder. Stick a toothpick through the roll to secure it; cut or break the toothpick so only a tiny bit sticks out (allowing the bacon to roll around and cook evenly).

Pour the canola oil into a deep skillet, and set over high heat. Sprinkle the chicken on all sides with half the salt. When the oil is very hot, lay the pieces, skin side down, in the skillet an inch or so apart—watch out for oil spatters. Don't crowd the chicken: if necessary, you can fry it in batches, cooking similar pieces together.

Drop the bacon rolls into the oil around the chicken, turning and shifting them often. Let the chicken fry in place for several minutes to brown on the underside, then turn and continue frying until the pieces are golden brown on all sides, 7 to 10 minutes or more. Fry the breast pieces only for

(recipe continues)

5 minutes or so, taking them out of the oil as soon as they are golden. Let the bacon rolls cook and get lightly crisp, but not dark. Adjust the heat to maintain steady sizzling and coloring; remove the crisped chicken pieces with tongs to a bowl.

Meanwhile, rinse and dry the potatoes; slice each one through the middle on the axis that gives the largest cut surface, then toss them in a bowl with the olive oil and the remaining salt.

When all the chicken and bacon is cooked and out of the skillet, pour off the frying oil. Return the skillet to medium heat, and put in all the potatoes, cut side down, in a single layer, pouring the olive oil into the skillet with them. Fry and crisp the potatoes for about 4 minutes to form a crust, then move them around the pan, still cut side down, until they're all brown and crisp, 7 minutes or more. Turn them over and fry another 2 minutes to cook and crisp on their rounded skin sides.

Keeping the skillet over medium heat, toss the onion wedges and rosemary branches around the pan, in with the potatoes. Return the chicken pieces—except the breast pieces—to the pan, along with the bacon rolls; pour in any chicken juices that have accumulated and add the cherry peppers. Raise the heat slightly, and carefully turn and tumble the chicken, potatoes, onions (and bacon and/or pepper pieces) so they are coated with pan juices, taking care not to break the potato pieces. Spread everything out in the pan—potatoes on the bottom as much as possible, to keep crisping up—and cover.

Lower the heat back to medium, and cook for about 7 minutes, shaking the pan occasionally; then uncover, and tumble the pieces and potatoes (and bacon rolls) again. Cover, and cook another 7 minutes or so, adding the breast pieces at this point. And give everything another tumble. Now cook covered for 10 minutes more.

Remove the cover, turn the pieces again, and cook in the open skillet for about 10 minutes, to evaporate the moisture and caramelize everything. Taste a bit of potato (or chicken) for salt, and sprinkle on more as needed. Turn the pieces now and then—when they are all glistening and golden, and the potatoes are cooked through, remove the skillet from the stove and—as I do at home—bring it right to the table.

ROASTED LOIN OF PORK STUFFED WITH PRUNES

Arrosto di Maiale alle Prugne

Roasted pork loin is always a great holiday centerpiece. It is delicious plain, or with herbs and rosemary, but I love the element of prunes paired with pork, especially if they are doused with grappa or bourbon. I use the prunes as a stuffing, and throw a few in the sauce as well. Much to my surprise, this has become an old favorite of my readers ever since they discovered it in *Lidia's Italian Table*—I believe it is the prunes that give the dish that something extra special that is so tasty and appealing, and demonstrate that the dinner is a special event.

SERVES 8

½ pound pitted prunes

½ cup bourbon

One boneless center pork-loin roast, about 3 pounds (ask your butcher to bone the rib roast, or you can do it yourself, and trim the fat)

10 fresh sage leaves

Salt and freshly ground black pepper

2 tablespoons extra-virgin olive oil

½ cup ¼-inch-dice carrots

½ cup ¼-inch-dice celery

½ cup roughly chopped onion

4 cloves garlic, crushed and peeled

2½ cups chicken stock or canned low-sodium chicken broth

In a small container, soak the prunes in bourbon for 1 hour.

Heat the oven to 450 degrees F. Drain the prunes, and set four of them aside along with the soaking liquid.

To stuff the roast: Use a sharp knife to cut a 1-inch pocket along the entire length of the eye, around the top half part of the roast. Cut from both sides of the roast until you cut through.

Line the remaining soaked prunes along the slit in the roast. Fold the flap over the opening, and tie the roast securely with kitchen twine at 2-inch intervals. Thread the sage leaves in two rows through the ties on either side of the roast. Season the roast generously with salt and pepper, and rub it with the olive oil. Place the roast in a large roasting pan. Roast 15 minutes.

Reduce the oven temperature to 400 degrees F. Tilt the roasting pan, and spoon off excess fat. Scatter the carrot, celery, onion, and garlic around the roast. Roast 15 minutes.

Add the reserved prunes and soaking liquid, and roast 10 minutes. Pour the stock into the pan,

(recipe continues)

and continue cooking, basting the roast occasionally with the pan juices, until a meat thermometer inserted into the thickest part of the roast registers 155 degrees F, 30 to 40 minutes.

Remove the roast to a platter. Pass the contents of the pan through a food mill fitted with the fine disc into a small bowl. (Alternatively, strain the liquid through a sieve, pressing on the vegetables to extract as much liquid as possible and to force some of the vegetables through the sieve.) Skim all fat from the surface of the sauce. The sauce should be thick enough to coat a spoon lightly. If not, transfer the sauce to a small saucepan, bring to a simmer, and simmer until it is thick enough. Season the sauce with salt and pepper, if needed. Cut the meat into ¼-inch slices, and serve with the sauce.

BRAISED PORK RIBS WITH RIGATONI

Costolette di Maiale Brasate con Rigatoni

America loves barbecued ribs, and I do as well, but Italians cook them in tomato sauce and dress their pasta with those delicious morsels of meat. The meat and sauce are absolutely succulent, and everybody at our home enjoys picking the meat off the bone.

SERVES 6

1 whole rack pork spare ribs (about 4 pounds)

Salt and freshly ground black pepper

¼ cup extra-virgin olive oil

2 large yellow onions, sliced (about 3 cups)

8 cloves garlic, peeled

6 pickled cherry peppers, stemmed, seeded, and quartered

Two 35-ounce cans Italian plum tomatoes (preferably San Marzano), with their liquid, seeded and crushed

2 fresh bay leaves, or 3 dried

6 sprigs fresh thyme

2 to 3 cups hot water, or as needed

1 pound rigatoni

¼ cup chopped fresh Italian parsley

⅔ cup freshly grated Grana Padano cheese, plus more for passing if you like

Cut the rack of spare ribs between the bones into single ribs (or ask your butcher to do this for you). Season the rib pieces with salt and pepper.

Heat the olive oil in a large, heavy braising pan over medium heat. Add as many of the ribs as will fit without touching. Cook, turning occasionally, until browned on all sides, about 10 minutes. Remove the ribs, and drain on a baking sheet lined with paper towel. Repeat with the remaining ribs. (Adjust the temperature throughout the browning so the fat in the pan is sizzling but the pieces of pork that stick to the pan don't burn.)

Pour off all but about 4 tablespoons of fat from the pan. Add the onions, garlic, and cherry peppers, and cook, stirring, until the onions are wilted and caramelized, about 4 minutes. Stir in the tomatoes, bay leaves, and thyme. Bring to a boil, scraping the pan to loosen the brown bits stuck to the bottom. Tuck the spare ribs into the tomato sauce, season lightly with salt and pepper, and bring to a boil. Adjust the heat so the liquid is simmering, and cook, turning the spare ribs in the sauce occasionally, until the ribs are fork-tender, about 2 hours. Ladle some of the hot water into the casserole from time to time, as necessary to keep the ribs covered with liquid.

(recipe continues)

To serve: When the ribs are almost tender, heat 6 quarts of salted water to a boil in an 8-quart pot. Stir the rigatoni into the boiling water, and cook, semi-covered, stirring occasionally, until done, about 10 minutes.

Drain the pasta, return it to the pot, and spoon in enough of the spare-rib sauce to coat the pasta generously. Toss in the parsley, and bring the sauce and pasta to a simmer, tossing to coat the pasta with sauce. Check the seasoning, adding salt and pepper if necessary. Remove the pot from the heat, and stir in the grated cheese. Transfer the pasta to a warm platter or individual plates, and top with the spare ribs. Spoon a little of the remaining sauce over the pasta, and serve immediately, passing additional sauce and grated cheese separately.

MEATLOAF WITH RICOTTA

Polpettone di Manzo con Ricotta

I am sure that your family has a favorite recipe for meatloaf—it is, after all, an American tradition. But the Italians have been making *polpettone* for many years. In the Italian version, ricotta is added to the mix, which renders the meatloaf tender and moist. All the e-mails I receive tell me this recipe has caught on like wildfire. To accompany this meatloaf, I love braised broccoli rabe or escarole, served on a separate plate or platter.

SERVES 8 OR MORE

1 cup milk

3 cups day old bread cubes from a loaf of country bread

3 pounds ground beef (freshly ground preferred)

3 large eggs, beaten with a pinch of salt

1 pound drained fresh ricotta (about 2 cups), plus more for the sauce if you like

1 bunch scallions, finely chopped (about 1 cup)

½ cup grated Grana Padano or Parmigiano-Reggiano cheese

¼ cup chopped fresh Italian parsley

½ teaspoon freshly grated nutmeg

1 tablespoon kosher salt

Freshly ground black pepper to taste

½ pound fresh mozzarella, cut into ½-inch cubes (about 2 cups)

¼ cup extra-virgin olive oil

4 to 5 cups Tomato Sauce (see page 103)

Preheat the oven to 375 degrees F.

Pour the milk over the bread cubes in a bowl, and let soak for a few minutes, until the bread is saturated. Squeeze the soft bread a handful at a time, pressing out as much milk as you can (discard the milk). Tear the bread into small shreds, and toss back into the empty bowl. Crumble the ground beef into the bowl, and add the eggs, ricotta, scallions, grated cheese, parsley, nutmeg, salt, and pepper. Fold and toss everything together, and squeeze the mixture a few times between your fingers to distribute all the ingredients evenly. Scatter the mozzarella cubes on top, and fold and mush them throughout the loaf mix.

Brush the roasting pan with 2 tablespoons of olive oil. Gather the meat mixture in the bowl, turn it into the pan, and shape it into a fat oval loaf the shape of a loaf of country bread. Drizzle with the remaining 2 tablespoons olive oil. Cover the pan with foil—tent it so it doesn't touch the meat—and bake 45 minutes. Remove the foil, and continue to bake until the meatloaf is browned all over and completely cooked through, another 1½ hours or so. (If you check the

(recipe continues)

loaf with a meat thermometer, it should reach a temperature of 160 degrees.) Remove the loaf from the oven, and let it rest for about 10 minutes.

Heat the tomato sauce to a simmer in a saucepan while the meat rests. Turn off the heat, and, if you like, stir ½ cup or so fresh ricotta into the sauce. Cut the loaf crosswise in the pan or on a cutting board, into slices as thick as you like.

Serve on warm dinner plates, topped with a spoonful or two of sauce, and pass more sauce at the table (or, for family-style serving, arrange the slices on a warm platter, topped with some of the sauce).

VEAL OSSOBUCO WITH BARLEY RISOTTO

Ossobuco di Vitello con Risotto d'Orzo

Ossobuco is the only dish that has not come off my menu at Felidia in thirty years. People absolutely love the rich flavor of veal shank prepared this way, and the soft meat, falling off the bone. The serious ossobuco eaters even scoop the marrow out of the center of the bones. I'm sure you have already tried several recipes for ossobuco if you're a fan, but do try this version—the juice from the orange keeps it light and fresh, but still very classic. The traditional ossobuco is usually served with risotto, as in the recipe in *Lidia Cooks from the Heart of Italy*, but I find that barley is much easier to handle. Unlike risotto, barley can be prepared in advance, and I love its nutty flavor. Here I also give you the recipe for the gremolata, a simple chopping of parsley, garlic, and lemon peel. It brings an additional freshness to the dish, but is not necessary.

SERVES 6

FOR THE OSSOBUCO

1 sprig fresh rosemary

1 sprig fresh thyme

2 fresh or dried bay leaves

4 whole cloves

1 lemon

1 orange, peel and juice

¼ cup extra-virgin olive oil

1 cup finely chopped onion

1 cup shredded carrots

1 cup finely diced celery

Salt and freshly ground black pepper to taste

3 whole veal shanks, bone-in, each about 3½ pounds, and each cut into 2 pieces

1 cup all-purpose flour

½ cup vegetable oil

1 tablespoon tomato paste

1 cup dry white wine

2 cups crushed canned plum tomatoes (preferably San Marzano)

4 cups chicken stock or canned low-sodium chicken broth

FOR THE BARLEY RISOTTO

2 quarts water

1 cup ¼-inch-dice carrots

1 cup ¼-inch-dice onion

1 cup ¼-inch-dice celery

2 fresh or dried bay leaves

1 teaspoon extra-virgin olive oil

1½ cups pearl barley

3 tablespoons unsalted butter

FOR THE GREMOLATA

Zest of 2 lemons (yellow part only, no white pith), finely chopped

¼ cup finely chopped fresh Italian parsley

1 clove garlic, finely chopped

(recipe continues)

Prepare the ossobuco: Tie the rosemary, thyme, bay leaves, and cloves securely in a 4-inch square of cheesecloth. With a vegetable peeler, remove the zest (yellow part of the peel only) from the lemon in wide strips. Do the same to the orange. Squeeze the juice from the orange, and reserve separately.

Heat the olive oil over medium heat in a wide, heavy casserole large enough to fit all the veal shanks. Add the onion, and cook, stirring occasionally, until wilted, about 5 minutes. Add the carrots, celery, and the cheesecloth bundle of herbs. Season lightly with salt, reduce the heat to low, and cook, stirring occasionally, for 10 minutes.

Pat the veal shanks dry with paper towels. Tie a piece of kitchen twine securely around the perimeter of each piece of shank to hold it together during cooking. Season them all with salt and pepper, and coat with flour, shaking the excess flour off. Divide the vegetable oil between two large, heavy skillets, and heat over medium heat. Add the shanks to the skillets, and cook, turning once, until well browned on all sides. (Alternatively, the shanks may be browned in batches in a single skillet.) Add the browned ossobuco to the casserole with the vegetables, and add the tomato paste. Stir the tomato paste into the vegetables, and cook, stirring occasionally and turning the shanks once or twice, 10 minutes. Pour in the white wine, bring to a boil, and then add the orange juice and the orange and lemon zest. Bring to a vigorous boil over high heat, and boil 10 minutes.

Add the crushed tomatoes; reduce the heat to low, and simmer, covered, for 30 minutes. Stir in a cup of the chicken stock. Cover, and simmer over low heat, adding stock to keep the level of liquid in the casserole the same, until the shanks are tender, about 1½ hours. Rotate the veal shanks in the casserole as they cook.

Meanwhile, prepare the barley and the gremolata: Bring the water, carrots, onion, celery, bay leaves, and olive oil to a boil. Stir in the barley, and cook until tender but still firm, about 40 minutes. Drain the barley, and set aside.

To make the gremolata, toss the lemon zest, parsley, and garlic in a small bowl until blended, and set aside.

When the veal is tender, remove the shank pieces and cut off the strings. Pass the cooking sauce through a sieve, pressing hard on the solids to remove as much liquid as possible. Return the meat and strained sauce to the casserole, and bring to a boil. Check the seasoning, and keep the veal warm over low heat.

Finish the barley: Heat the butter in a large, heavy skillet over medium-low heat. Add the barley, and cook, stirring often, until it is heated through and coated with butter. Season with salt and pepper.

Serve some barley and two pieces of the veal on each plate, sprinkling the veal with gremolata.

SCALOPPINE SALTIMBOCCA, ROMAN STYLE, WITH SAUTÉED SPINACH

Saltimbocca alla Romana, con Spinaci Saltati

Veal scaloppine are traditionally used in this recipe, but chicken breast or pork will work just as well. The beauty of this is that it is easy, flavorful, and a complete dish, with vegetables and proteins.

SERVES 4

FOR THE SAUTÉED SPINACH

1 pound loose spinach, or one 10-ounce cellophane package spinach

2 tablespoons extra-virgin olive oil

3 cloves garlic, peeled

Salt and freshly ground black pepper to taste

FOR THE SCALOPPINE

Salt and freshly ground black pepper to taste

Eight 3-ounce slices veal, lightly pounded to about ⅛ inch thick

4 slices (about 2 ounces total) imported Italian prosciutto, each slice cut in half crosswise

8 large fresh sage leaves

All-purpose flour for dredging

3 tablespoons extra-virgin olive oil, or as needed

6 tablespoons unsalted butter

¼ cup dry white wine

1 cup chicken stock or canned low-sodium chicken broth

Wash the spinach, but don't dry the leaves completely. The water that clings to them will steam the spinach as it cooks.

Heat the olive oil in a wide skillet over medium heat. Whack the garlic cloves with the side of a knife, and toss them into the oil; cook, shaking the pan, until golden, about 2 minutes. Scatter the spinach a large handful at a time into the pan, season lightly with salt and pepper, and cover the pan. Cook until the spinach begins to release its liquid. Uncover the pan, and cook, stirring, until the spinach is wilted and its water has evaporated, 1 to 3 minutes. Taste, and season with additional salt and pepper if necessary. Remove from heat, and cover the pan to keep it warm while you prepare the saltimbocca.

Season the scaloppine lightly with salt and pepper (keeping in mind that the prosciutto is already cured with salt). Cover each scaloppina with a half slice of the prosciutto; tap the prosciutto with the back of a knife so it adheres well to the meat. Center a sage leaf over the prosciutto, and fasten it in place with a toothpick, weaving the toothpick in and out as if you were taking a stitch.

Dredge the scaloppine in the flour to coat both sides lightly, then shake off excess flour. Heat the olive oil and 2 tablespoons of the butter in a large, heavy skillet over medium heat until the butter is foaming. Slip as many of the scaloppine, prosciutto side down, into the pan as fit without touching. Cook just until the prosciutto is light golden, about 2 minutes. Turn, and cook until the second side is browned, about 2 minutes. Remove, and drain on paper towels. Repeat with the remaining scaloppine, adding more oil if necessary.

Remove all the scaloppine from the skillet, and pour off the oil. Return the pan to the heat, and pour in the wine. Add the remaining butter, and cook until the wine is reduced by about half. Pour in the chicken stock, and bring to a vigorous boil. Tuck the scaloppine into the sauce. Simmer until the sauce is reduced and lightly thickened, about 3 to 4 minutes. Taste, and season with salt and pepper if necessary.

To serve, spoon the spinach into a mound in the center of each plate. Arrange two pieces of the saltimbocca over the spinach. Spoon some of the pan sauce over the scaloppine, and serve immediately.

VEAL CHOPS WITH FONTINA

Costolette alla Fontina

Veal chops are always something special and extravagant, but worth spending the money on when prepared well. In this recipe, thick rib chops are stuffed with Fontina cheese, browned and braised on the stovetop, then baked. The result is quite grand, because the succulent meat and pan sauce are enriched with driblets and hidden pockets of sweet melted Fontina. However, let me point out that you can make *costolette alla Fontina* in more modest versions that are absolutely delicious and much easier on the pocketbook, using thick pork chops or plump chicken breasts. You may have to adjust both the amount of cheese you put inside and the cooking time at each step to avoid overcooking.

SERVES 6

6 bone-in veal rib chops, about 1½ inches thick, 8 to 10 ounces each

2 teaspoons kosher salt

8 ounces shredded Italian Fontina (a good white cheddar will do as well)

1 cup grated Grana Padano or Parmigiano-Reggiano cheese

4 tablespoons butter

1 tablespoon extra-virgin olive oil

½ cup all-purpose flour for dredging, plus more as needed

12 fresh sage leaves

1 tablespoon tomato paste

2 cups white wine

½ cup hot chicken broth

Arrange an oven rack to accommodate a covered saucepan, and heat oven to 400 degrees F.

Trim the chops, leaving only a thin layer of fat on the perimeter. With a sharp, thin knife, slice horizontally into the outer edge of each chop, splitting the meaty portion in two almost all the way to the bone, forming a pocket for stuffing. With the mallet, pound individually each flap of the chop meat, spreading the meat apart, flattening it to ½-inch thickness. When all the chops are sliced and pounded, salt them on both sides, using a teaspoon in all. In a bowl, toss together the shredded Fontina and the grated Grana Padano or Parmigiano-Reggiano, and divide the cheeses into six equal portions. One at a time, lightly compress the cheese portions into oval patties, and slip them into the sliced chop pockets. Fold the bottom meat flap over the top flap—enclosing the cheese—and thread a toothpick through both flaps to keep them together.

Put 2 tablespoons of the butter and the olive oil in a large skillet, and set over medium-high heat. Spread the flour on a plate, dredge each chop on both sides, shake off excess flour, and lay the chop in the pan. When all the chops are in the pan, drop the sage leaves in between them. Cook the chops for 5 minutes or more, turning them once or twice, until well browned on both sides. Clear a space in the pan bottom, drop in the tomato paste, and toast it in the hot spot for a minute. Pour the wine over the tomato paste, stir them together, and shake the pan to distribute the liquid. Bring it to a boil, and cook for 3 minutes or so, to reduce.

Add the remaining butter, and whisk it into the pan liquid. Turn the chops over, pour in the chicken broth, sprinkle on the remaining salt, and bring to a boil. Cover the pan, and place in the oven. Roast for about 15 minutes, then remove the cover and roast another 10 minutes or so, until the chops are done and the sauce has thickened. Remove from the oven, and place the chops on a warm platter. If the sauce is thin, put the pan over high heat and reduce until the sauce has the consistency you like.

Serve right away—while the cheese is still oozing—arranging all the chops on a warm platter and spooning the sauce over, family-style, or on warm dinner plates with mashed potatoes alongside and sauce drizzled over.

BRAISED BEEF ROLLS

Braciole di Manzo

A big pot of sauce with plenty of beef braciole perking on a stove—that has been the Sunday meal for many Italian American households for as long as I can remember. Sausages and meatballs added to the pot have sometimes made for an even more bountiful dinner. The braciole are served on a platter, while the sauce dresses a big bowl of rigatoni. The only thing left to do is to beckon everybody to the table to eat.

SERVES 6

FOR THE BRACIOLE

1½ cups milk

2 cups ½-inch bread cubes, cut from day-old Italian bread with crusts removed

2 hard-cooked eggs, peeled and coarsely chopped

¼ cup chopped fresh Italian parsley

¼ cup freshly grated Grana Padano or Parmigiano-Reggiano cheese

¼ cup raisins

¼ cup pine nuts, toasted

1 clove garlic, finely chopped

2 pounds beef bottom round, cut into 12 slices each about ½ inch thick

12 slices imported Italian prosciutto (about 6 ounces)

¼ pound imported provola or provolone cheese, cut into ¼-by-¼-by-1-inch sticks

Salt and freshly ground black pepper

FOR THE SAUCE

One 35-ounce can Italian plum tomatoes (preferably San Marzano)

3 tablespoons extra-virgin olive oil

2 small onions (about 8 ounces), chopped

2 cloves garlic, finely chopped

½ cup dry red wine

3 tablespoons tomato paste

2 fresh or dried bay leaves

Salt and hot red pepper flakes to taste

To make the stuffing: Pour the milk into a medium bowl, add the bread cubes, and let soak until the bread is very soft, 20 to 30 minutes. Drain the bread, squeeze out excess milk from the cubes with your hands, and return bread to the bowl. Stir in the chopped eggs, parsley, Grana Padano or Parmigiano-Reggiano, raisins, pine nuts, and garlic. Mix well, and set aside.

With the toothed side of a heavy meat mallet, pound each slice of beef round to a thickness of about ¼ inch. Arrange one of the pounded meat slices in front of you with one of the short sides closest to you. Top with a slice of prosciutto, and tap the prosciutto with the back side of a knife so it adheres to the beef. Spread 2 tablespoons of the stuffing over the beef slice, leaving a 1-inch border around the

(recipe continues)

edges. Place a stick of provolone crosswise over the edge of the stuffing closest to you. Fold the border over the provolone, then fold the side borders in to overlap the edges of the stuffing. Roll into a compact tube. Secure the end flap with a toothpick. Repeat with the remaining beef and stuffing, then season the rolls with salt and pepper.

Empty the tomatoes into a bowl, and squeeze them with your hands until coarsely crushed, removing the cores as you do.

Heat the olive oil in a large, heavy casserole over medium heat. Stir in the onions and garlic, and cook until the onions are wilted, about 5 minutes. Add as many of the braciole as will fit in a single layer, and cook, turning the braciole as necessary, until golden on all sides, about 7 minutes. If necessary, repeat with any remaining braciole. Adjust the heat under the pan as necessary to prevent the beef from scorching.

Pour the wine into the casserole, bring to a boil, and cook until most of it has evaporated. Stir in the tomatoes, and bring to a boil. Add tomato paste and bay leaves, and stir until the paste is dissolved. Season lightly with salt and red pepper flakes, adjust the heat so the liquid is simmering, and cook, adding water as necessary to keep the braciole completely submerged, until the beef is tender, about 3 hours.

Remove the toothpicks before serving. The braciole can be prepared up to 2 days in advance, then warmed over low heat until heated through.

PAN-SEARED STEAK WITH PIZZAIOLA SAUCE

Bistecca alla Pizzaiola

The tomato sauce and vegetables in this dish will bring to mind the flavors of pizza, an American favorite. And when those flavors are paired with steak, another American favorite, how could you go wrong? I always enjoy a good grilled steak, but the sauce and earthiness of the vegetables here make for a perfect pairing with the meat and a good piece of crusty bread to mop up the leftover sauce on your plate.

SERVES 4

3 tablespoons extra-virgin olive oil

3 cloves garlic, peeled and sliced

1 red bell pepper, cored and seeded, cut into 1-inch strips

1 yellow bell pepper, cored and seeded, cut into 1-inch strips

2 cups sliced white button mushrooms

1¼ teaspoons kosher salt

½ teaspoon dried oregano

One 14-ounce can Italian plum tomatoes (preferably San Marzano), crushed by hand

Four 8-ounce bone-in shell steaks, about 1 inch thick

Heat the olive oil in a large skillet over medium-high heat. When the oil is hot, add the sliced garlic. Let the garlic sizzle a minute, then toss in the bell peppers and mushrooms. Season with 1 teaspoon of the salt and the oregano. Sauté until the mushrooms and peppers are caramelized on the edges, about 5 minutes.

Pour in the tomatoes, and slosh out the can with ½ cup hot water, adding that to the skillet as well. Bring to a simmer, and cook, uncovered, until the sauce is thickened and the peppers break down, about 12 to 15 minutes.

Season the steaks with the remaining ¼ teaspoon salt. Sear the steaks in a large cast-iron skillet over high heat until done to your liking, about 2 minutes per side for rare. Let the steaks rest for a few minutes while the sauce finishes cooking.

To serve, put the steaks on plates and top with the pepper sauce. Serve immediately.

BEEF BRAISED IN BAROLO

Stuffato al Barolo

Even if you are thousands of miles away, there's no doubt you will be transported to northern Italy for a few hours while the beef in this recipe cooks to melting tenderness. And even though in Italy—specifically, in Piemonte—it is braised in Barolo wine, this dish is delicious when any good full-bodied red wine is used in cooking it.

SERVES 6 OR MORE

5-pound boneless beef roast, flat iron, chuck, or bottom round, trimmed of fat

2 teaspoons coarse sea salt or kosher salt, or to taste

⅓ cup extra-virgin olive oil

2 medium onions (1 pound total), peeled and quartered

3 medium carrots (½ pound total), peeled and cut into 2-inch wedges

4 medium stalks celery (½ pound total), cut into 2-inch chunks

6 plump cloves garlic, peeled

2 branches fresh rosemary with lots of needles

6 large fresh sage leaves

¼ teaspoon freshly grated nutmeg

1 teaspoon whole black peppercorns

1 ounce dried porcini slices (about 1 cup, loosely packed)

2 bottles Barolo (750 ml each), or as needed

2 cups beef stock, or as needed

Heat the oven to 250 degrees F with a rack set in the center.

Season all surfaces of the roast with half the salt. Pour the olive oil into a large, heavy braiser and set over medium-high heat. Lay the roast in, and brown it until caramelized all over. Remove to a platter.

While keeping the skillet over medium-high heat, drop in the cut vegetables and garlic cloves, toss to coat with oil, and spread them out in the pan. Drop in the rosemary, sage leaves, grated nutmeg, peppercorns, dried porcini, and remaining teaspoon salt, and toss all together. Cook for 3 or 4 minutes, stirring frequently and scraping up the browned meat bits on the pan bottom, just until the vegetables soften; then lower the heat.

Push the vegetables to the sides and return the roast to the pan, laying it flat on the bottom. Pour in the bottles of wine and any meat juices that collected on the platter. The roast should be at least half submerged—add beef stock as needed.

Cover the pot, and heat until the wine is steaming but not boiling. Uncover the pan, and place it in the oven. After 30 minutes, rotate the roast so the exposed meat is now submerged in the braising liquid. Braise this way, turning the meat in the pan every 30 minutes, for about 3 hours, until fork-tender. The liquid should not boil—if it does, pour in some cold water to stop the bubbling, and lower the oven temperature.

After 2½ hours, check the beef. It should be fork tender. Take the pan from the oven. Move the meat to a platter, and reserve intact carrot and celery pieces to use as a garnish.

Skim any fat from the braising juices, heat to a boil, and reduce to a saucy consistency that coats the back of a spoon. Pour through a sieve set over a clean container. Press the juices from the strained herbs and vegetable pieces. Pour in any juices from the meat platter, and season the sauce to taste with salt and freshly ground black pepper. (If you are not going to serve it right away, put the meat and reserved vegetables in the sauce to rest and cool, for a couple of hours or overnight in the refrigerator.)

To serve, slice the meat crosswise (easiest when it is cool). Pour a shallow layer of sauce in a wide skillet, and lay the slices in, overlapping. Heat the sauce to bubbling, spooning it over the beef, so the slices are lightly coated. Lift them with a broad spatula and slide onto a warm platter, fanned out. Heat the carrots and celery in the sauce, too, if you've saved them, and arrange on the platter. Serve, passing more heated sauce at the table.

DESSERTS

ALMOND PINE NUT COOKIES

Amaretti con Pinoli

These cookies appear at every Italian holiday. They are simple to make, keep well for a week or more, are a great gift to give and to receive, but most of all they are delicious. Some like them chewy, some like them crunchy; the degree of crunchiness is only a matter of how long you bake them. The longer you bake them the crunchier they become.

MAKES ABOUT 30 COOKIES

Two 7-ounce tubes almond paste

1 cup sugar

2 large egg whites

Zest of 1 orange, finely grated

1½ cups pine nuts, left whole

Preheat oven to 350 degrees F. Line two baking sheets with parchment.

Crumble the almond paste into the work bowl of a food processor, and process until the paste is in fine crumbs. Sprinkle in the sugar with the motor running. Once the sugar is incorporated, add the egg whites and orange zest. Process to make a smooth dough, about 20 to 30 seconds.

Spread the pine nuts on a plate. Form the dough into 2-tablespoon-size balls, roll and press them to coat in pine nuts, then place them on the baking sheets. Bake in the upper and lower third of the oven, switching trays halfway through baking, until lightly golden and springy to the touch, about 13 to 15 minutes. Let cool on the baking sheets for about 5 minutes, then transfer the cookies to cooling racks to cool completely.

ROASTED PEARS AND GRAPES

Pere e Uva al Forno

This is my favorite dessert for a dinner party. Light, tasty, and easy to make, it is a great dessert when you have company: you can just slip this recipe into the oven and have a grand dessert, especially if you serve it with vanilla ice cream. Pears and grapes make a great marriage of flavors, but, depending on the season, I also like baked quince and cranberries. To try that, cut the peeled and cored quince in quarters, because they take longer than the pears to bake, then add the cranberries instead of the grapes.

SERVES 6

2 cups seedless red grapes

1 cup sugar

Juice of 2 lemons

⅔ cup Moscato wine

½ vanilla pod, split lengthwise

2 tablespoons apricot jam

3 firm but ripe Bosc pears

Preheat oven to 375 degrees F. Place the grapes in a baking dish. Combine the sugar, lemon juice, Moscato, vanilla beans from the pod, and apricot jam in a bowl, and stir until blended. Pour this over the grapes. Cut each pear in half through the core, and remove the cores and seeds. Nestle the pear halves, cut side up, into the grapes.

Bake until the pears are tender and the liquid around the grapes is thick and syrupy, about 50 minutes. Remove the pears, and let stand for about 10 minutes. Serve them with some of the grapes and their liquid spooned around them.

CHOCOLATE BISCOTTI PUDDING

Budino di Gianduia

This delightful pudding is a fine example of the art of using leftovers to make something fresh and new. Here crumbled biscotti, chopped chocolate, and chopped hazelnuts are mixed into the warm custard. "Chocolate" and "custard" are two favorite words at my house, and here you get to have them both.

SERVES 6 TO 8

2 large eggs

¾ cup sugar

2 tablespoons cornstarch

1¼ cups heavy cream, plus more for whipped topping

1 cup milk

⅓ cup cocoa powder

1½ cups coarsely hand-crumbled plain biscotti

3½ ounces finely chopped bittersweet chocolate

½ cup toasted, skinned, finely chopped hazelnuts, plus crushed nuts for topping (optional)

Whisk the eggs with the sugar in a large bowl. Whisk the cornstarch into the eggs until no lumps remain.

Pour the cream and milk into a saucepan, set it over low heat, and bring to a simmer. Turn off the heat, and slowly pour about 1 cup of the hot milk-cream into the egg bowl, whisking steadily, to temper the eggs. When blended, slowly pour the tempered eggs back into the saucepan of warm milk and cream, again whisking constantly. Set the pan back over medium-low heat, and whisk steadily until the custard heats and thickens. Don't let it boil, though it should bubble occasionally. Cook for 7 to 8 minutes, until it is quite thick.

Sift cocoa powder.

Remove the custard from the heat, and stir in the crumbled biscotti, chopped chocolate, nuts, and cocoa powder. Stir continuously until the chocolate has melted and all the ingredients are evenly blended.

Line a 9-inch pie plate with plastic wrap, leaving a few inches' overhang on all edges. Pour the custard into the pie plate, and cover with plastic wrap, laying it directly on top of the pudding. Refrigerate until set, at least 4 hours or overnight.

To serve: Remove the top sheet of plastic, invert the budino onto a serving plate, and cut into wedges. Top with unsweetened whipped cream, and coarsely crumbled biscotti (if you have any left) or crushed hazelnuts.

APPLE STRUDEL

Strudel di Mele

This favorite is dedicated to my brother, Franco, and my son-in-law, Corrado. I always make it at a family meal in the fall, when the apples are in season, and I know they will both be there.

Strudel is a Middle European dessert that is very common in the Italian region of Friuli–Venezia Giulia and on the peninsula of Istria, where I grew up. But strudel is loved everywhere, especially at our restaurant Becco, where it is served warm with vanilla sauce and cinnamon ice cream. I make many variations on the theme, sometimes by adding fresh cranberries and/or squash to the apples. Like the strudel recipes in *Lidia's Family Table*, that makes it a very seasonal Thanksgiving treat.

SERVES 10

FOR THE DOUGH

2 cups sifted unbleached all-purpose flour, plus more for kneading the dough

3 tablespoons extra-virgin olive oil

½ teaspoon salt

½ cup lukewarm water, or as needed

FOR THE FILLING

1 cup golden raisins

2 tablespoons dark rum

1 lemon

½ cup (1 stick) unsalted butter, softened, cut into tablespoons

1 cup plain dry breadcrumbs

1½ cups granulated sugar

½ teaspoon ground cinnamon

3 pounds tart green apples, such as Granny Smith

Olive oil for the pan and brushing the strudel

Confectioners' sugar for dusting

In a small bowl, toss the raisins with the rum. Let them stand, tossing occasionally, while preparing the strudel.

To make the dough: Combine the flour, oil, and salt in the work bowl of a food processor. With the motor running, add ½ cup water and process until the mixture forms a smooth, silky dough. (If the mixture is too dry, add more water, 1 tablespoon at a time.) Turn the dough out onto a lightly floured surface and knead, adding flour as necessary to prevent the dough from sticking, until the dough is very smooth and elastic, about 3 minutes. Wrap the dough in plastic wrap, and let it rest at room temperature for 2 to 3 hours or in the refrigerator for up to 2 days. (Let the refrigerated dough sit at room temperature for at least 1 hour before rolling it.)

Use a fine grater to remove the zest from the lemon. Squeeze the juice from the lemon, strain it if necessary, and combine the juice and zest in a medium-size mixing bowl.

Melt half the butter in a medium-size skillet over

(recipe continues)

medium heat. Add the breadcrumbs and toast, stirring constantly, until lightly browned, about 5 minutes. Remove the skillet from the heat, and stir in ½ cup of the sugar and the cinnamon.

Add the remaining cup of granulated sugar and the rum and raisins to the bowl with the lemon juice and zest.

Peel the apples, and cut them into ½-inch-thick wedges, cutting away the seeds and cores and adding the wedges to the bowl of the lemon-sugar mixture (to prevent them from darkening). Let the apples stand, tossing occasionally, until the sugar begins to dissolve and the apples are coated with the syrup.

Preheat the oven to 450 degrees F and brush a large baking pan with olive oil.

Lightly flour a large, smooth wooden or marble surface. Using a rolling pin, roll out the dough from the center to the edges into a very thin rectangle 2 feet by 1½ feet. As it gets thinner, you should be able to pull and stretch it gently with your hands to coax it into the shape you want. Don't worry if the dough tears a little in spots—you can patch it later—or if it doesn't form a perfect rectangle.

Turn the dough so one of the longer sides is facing you. Under the end of the dough across from you place a kitchen towel or length of double-thick cheesecloth under the entire side of the dough rectangle and extending about 4 inches beyond it. (This will help you move the strudel to the baking sheet once it is formed.) Spread the breadcrumb mixture evenly over the dough, leaving a clean 1½-inch-wide border on all sides of the rectangle. Dot the bread-

crumbs with small pieces of the remaining ¼ cup of butter.

Arrange the apple mixture in a long mound along the side closest to you. The mound of apples should measure about 4 inches wide and as long as the breadcrumb mixture, leaving the 1½-inch-wide border clean. Fold the clean border closest to you over the apples. Begin rolling the strudel into a fairly tight roll, starting at one end of the apple mound, giving it a half-roll, and gradually working your way down the roll. Don't worry if the roll is uneven or tears in places. You should end up with a fairly even, lumpy-looking roll that is centered, seam side down, on the kitchen towel. Use the towel to transfer the strudel to the prepared baking sheet, bending the strudel into a crescent shape if necessary to fit it on the pan.

Cut off any excess dough from the ends. Seal the ends of the strudel by folding the ends of the roll underneath and pressing them firmly with your fingers. Brush the strudel lightly with olive oil, and place it in the oven; then immediately reduce the oven temperature to 375 degrees F. Bake 30 minutes, until the top of the strudel is a light golden brown. (If it's deeper in color than that, reduce the temperature to 350 degrees F.) Rotate the baking pan in the oven so the strudel cooks evenly, and continue to bake until the strudel crust is deep golden brown and firm, about 30 minutes more.

Remove the strudel from the oven, and let stand until completely cooled. To serve, cut the strudel into 1-inch-thick slices and sprinkle them with confectioners' sugar.

BLUEBERRY APRICOT FRANGIPANE TART

Crostata di Mirtilli ed Albiccoche al Frangipane

Almonds are a favorite ingredient in Italian baking, and frangipane is a batter made of almond flour that, when baked in a shell and studded with blueberries, takes on the texture of a tart with an almond custard holding a fruit center. For this recipe you can buy apricot glaze, but to make your own, heat apricot jam in a small saucepan over low heat. If the jam is chunky, add a tablespoon or two of water, and strain before using.

MAKES ONE 10-INCH TART, SERVING ABOUT 8

FOR THE SHELL

1½ cups all-purpose flour

¼ cup sugar

½ teaspoon baking powder

Pinch of salt

½ cup (1 stick) unsalted butter, cut into cherry-size pieces and chilled

1 large egg yolk

Zest of 1 lemon, grated

Ice water as needed

FOR THE FILLING

½ cup (1 stick) unsalted butter, softened, plus more for the pan

⅓ cup sugar

2 large eggs

1 cup almond flour

1 teaspoon vanilla extract

½ cup apricot glaze

1 cup fresh blueberries

½ pound ripe apricots, halved and pitted, or one 24-ounce can apricot halves, drained

Make the shell: Sift the flour, sugar, baking powder, and salt together into a bowl. Add the butter, egg yolk, and lemon zest, and work the ingredients together with your fingers until the butter resembles cornflakes and is distributed evenly throughout the flour mixture. Sprinkle 3 tablespoons ice water over the mixture, and toss lightly just until the dough holds together when lightly pressed. If necessary, add a little more ice water. Wrap the dough in plastic wrap, and let rest in the refrigerator for 1 hour.

Butter a 10-inch tart pan with a removable bottom. Roll out the dough to a 12-inch circle of even thickness. Center the dough over the tart pan, fit the dough well into the edges with your fingers, and trim off excess overhanging dough. Prick the bottom of the tart shell with a fork, and set on a baking sheet in the freezer for 10 minutes.

Meanwhile, preheat the oven to 350 degrees F.

Make the filling: With an electric mixer at medium

speed, cream the butter with the sugar until fluffy, about 3 minutes. Add the eggs one at a time, beating well after each addition. Add the almond flour and vanilla, and mix until a smooth batter forms.

Brush the tart shell with ¼ cup of warm apricot glaze, then spread the blueberries over the bottom. Pour the almond-flour mixture over the blueberries, and with a spatula spread it evenly. Arrange the apricot halves over the almond-flour mixture, cut side down. Place the tart in the oven, and bake until the almond-flour mixture and the edges of the tart shell are golden brown, about 40 minutes.

Let the tart cool for 30 minutes, then brush with the remaining ¼ cup warm apricot glaze.

PLUM TART

Crostata di Prugne

I absolutely love a fruit tart, any fruit tart; it is my favorite dessert. Prune tarts in particular appeal to me—Grandma had several plum trees, whose fruit she dried into prunes for the winter; dried or fresh, they were one of my favorite fruits. But certainly this crostata can turn into a favorite for every season by changing the fruit; cherries, peaches, apricots, pears, and apples are only a few options.

SERVES 8

¼ cup smooth apricot jam

One 10-inch tart shell, prebaked for 15 minutes

14 firm, ripe purple plums, halved and pitted

2 tablespoons sugar

½ tablespoon water

¼ tablespoon lemon juice

Preheat the oven to 350 degrees F.

Brush 3 tablespoons of the apricot jam over the bottom of the prebaked tart shell. Starting from the outside edge of the shell, arrange the plums cut side up in concentric circles until the shell is filled. Bake the tart 10 minutes, sprinkle the sugar over the plums, and return to the oven for an additional 25 to 35 minutes or longer, depending on the texture of the plums, until the pastry is nicely browned and the plums are well cooked. If the pastry gets brown before the plums cook, cover with foil and continue to bake until plums are done. Remove from the oven and cool.

Melt the remaining apricot jam in a small saucepan, stirring in the water and lemon juice. (Strain if the jam is lumpy.) When the tart has cooled somewhat, brush the plums with the apricot glaze. Serve at room temperature.

RICOTTA CHEESECAKE

Torta di Ricotta

Cheesecake is a favorite in every household, but even the most dedicated cheesecake aficionados have to admit that Italian ricotta cheesecake is something special. The recipe is simple and basic. It is not the creamy cream-cheese cake you might be used to—it has a crumbly texture and can be a bit wet at times—but it is the cheesecake of the Italians. Though I love serving it warm, it is good cold as well.

SERVES 8

3½ cups ricotta

½ cup raisins

3 tablespoons dark rum

Softened butter and fine dry breadcrumbs for the pan

5 large eggs, separated

¾ cup sugar

Pinch of salt

Zest of 1 large lemon, grated

Zest of 1 large orange, grated

½ cup heavy cream

½ cup pine nuts

Place the ricotta in a cheesecloth-lined sieve, and place the sieve over a bowl. Cover the ricotta with plastic wrap, and place in the refrigerator for at least 8 hours and up to 1 day.

Soak the raisins in rum in a small bowl, tossing occasionally, until the raisins are softened and have absorbed most of the rum, about 30 minutes.

Brush an 8-inch springform pan with enough softened butter to coat it lightly. Sprinkle the breadcrumbs over the butter to coat generously. Shake out the excess crumbs. Preheat the oven to 375 degrees F.

Beat the egg yolks, sugar, and salt in a large bowl with a whisk until pale yellow. Add the drained ricotta and the lemon and orange zest, and beat until blended thoroughly. Beat in the cream. Fold in the pine nuts, and the raisins and rum, with a rubber spatula, blending well. Beat the egg whites in a separate bowl with a hand mixer or wire whisk until they form firm peaks when a beater is lifted from them. Add about one-fourth of the egg whites to the ricotta mixture, and gently stir it in. Add the remaining egg whites, and fold them in, using a large rubber spatula to scrape the batter from the bottom of the bowl up and over the whites. Pour the cake mixture into the prepared pan, and bake until the cake is golden brown on top and set in the center, about 1 hour and 10 minutes.

Cool the cake completely before removing the sides of the pan. Serve the cake at room temperature or chilled.

CANNOLI NAPOLEONS

Cannolo a Strati

Traditional cannoli are crispy fried dough cylinders stuffed with ricotta cream. This version is made with deep-fried discs of cannoli, stacked high with layers of ricotta cream in between, just like a napoleon. It is a much easier technique, frying the discs rather than the tubular cannoli shells, and the finished cannoli taste as good as the traditional version but look quite contemporary.

MAKES 6 TO 8 CANNOLI NAPOLEONS

FOR THE PASTRY DOUGH

1½ cups all-purpose flour, plus more for rolling

2 tablespoons granulated sugar

¼ teaspoon salt

2 tablespoons extra-virgin olive oil

1 teaspoon white vinegar

½ cup dry red wine, or as needed

FOR THE CANNOLI CREAM

1 pound (2 cups) fresh ricotta

⅔ cup confectioners' sugar, plus more for decoration

1 tablespoon Grand Marnier (optional, but very good!)

1 ounce unsweetened chocolate (or 3 tablespoons bittersweet chips)

2 tablespoons candied orange rind

2 tablespoons almonds, toasted

1 cup vegetable oil, or as needed

Honey and grated chocolate for decoration

To make the dough: Put the flour, granulated sugar, and salt in a food-processor bowl, and process just to mix. Mix the olive oil, vinegar, and wine together in a measuring cup, and, with the machine running, pour all but 1 tablespoon of the liquid in; process for 20 seconds or so, until a dough gathers on the blade. If it feels hard and dry, sprinkle in the remaining liquid and process briefly, to make it moist and malleable. Turn the dough out of the bowl, scraping any bits from the sides and blade, and knead by hand into a soft, smooth ball. Flatten to a disc, wrap very tightly in plastic, and refrigerate for up to 2 days. Make the pastry dough in the food processor a day or two—or at least 4 hours—in advance for the best texture.

To make the cannoli cream: Put the fresh ricotta in a fine-meshed sieve, and set it inside a bowl to drain for 12 to 24 hours in advance. Cover the ricotta with plastic wrap, and refrigerate.

Whip the ricotta with the whisk attachment of an electric mixer until smooth. Whip in the confectioners' sugar and Grand Marnier. Chop the chocolate (or chips) into coarse bits—big enough to bite into and to be visible. Coarsely chop the candied peel and almonds to the same size, about the size of

(recipe continues)

raisins. Fold the chopped pieces into the cream; refrigerate until you assemble the cannoli.

Cut the pastry dough in half. On a lightly floured surface, roll out one piece of dough to a rectangle 11 by 14 inches (or as close as possible). Use a round cookie cutter about 3 inches in diameter to cut discs. Set the rounds aside, on a lightly floured tray, to rest for 15 minutes before frying. Meanwhile, roll out and cut the remaining half of the dough the same way.

To fry the pastry, pour vegetable oil into a skillet to a depth of ¼ inch, and set over medium heat. Use the point of a small, sharp knife to pierce each pastry round about ten times all over its surface, as though you were making pinpricks through the dough. (These tiny holes will prevent the pastry from ballooning when fried.)

Heat the oil until the edge of the dough sizzles gently when dipped into it, then lay in as many rounds as you can, 2 inches apart. Raise the heat to keep the oil temperature up (but lower it as soon as the sizzling gets too fast). Fry the rounds for about 3 minutes on the first side, pushing them under the oil occasionally to heat the top surface. As the tops begin to bubble, press with tongs to prevent big bubbles from ballooning—small bubbles are OK. When the bottom is golden brown, flip the rounds over and fry until evenly colored and crisp on both sides, about 2 more minutes. As soon as they're done, lift them with tongs, let excess oil drip off, and lay them to drain on folded paper towels. Fry all the rounds this way, adding oil as needed and heating it between batches.

Assemble your cannoli napoleons: Set one round on the plate, drop about 1½ tablespoons of cannoli cream in the center, lay another round on top—sides aligned—and press gently to spread the cream. Drop on another layer of cream, cover with a third round, and press. Finally, shower the top of each napoleon with confectioners' sugar and embellish with drizzles of honey or a sprinkle of finely grated chocolate and serve.

CRÊPES WITH CHOCOLATE AND WALNUTS

Palacinke

Truly no different from crespelle or crêpes, *palacinke* is the name I first used to ask for these delicious thin pancakes. My mother would whip them up for dinner; she often served them with only a sprinkle of sugar, or adorned them with preserves like rose-hip jam, apricot marmalade, or prune butter. As a child I loved them with any of those fillings, but the most luxurious—and always our favorite—were *palacinke* topped with melted chocolate. This is, hands down, the favorite dessert of my grandchildren. They can fill, roll, and eat them faster than I can cook them, and I usually lose count.

MAKES A DOZEN *PALACINKE,* SERVING 6

2 eggs

2 cups water

1 tablespoon dark rum

1 teaspoon vanilla extract

2 tablespoons sugar, plus more to sweeten whipped cream if desired

⅓ teaspoon salt

2 cups flour

8 tablespoons butter, melted, or more as needed

Zest of 2 lemons, finely grated

10 ounces excellent bittersweet or semisweet chocolate (12 ounces or more for extreme chocolate-lovers)

1 cup heavy cream, chilled

1½ cups walnuts, toasted and coarsely chopped

To make the batter, whisk together the eggs, water, rum, vanilla, sugar, and salt in a large bowl until well blended. Sift the flour on top, a bit at a time, whisking each addition until smooth. Drizzle in half the melted butter, whisking until the batter has slightly thickened into the consistency of melted ice cream. Finally, whisk in the lemon zest. Put the remaining butter in a small cup and keep it warm.

Break or chop the chocolate into small pieces, and put them a bowl set in a pan of hot (not boiling) water. When the chocolate begins to melt, stir until completely smooth, and keep it warm, in the water, off the heat.

Set a crêpe pan or skillet over medium-high heat until quite hot. Pour in a couple tablespoons of butter, quickly swirl it all over the pan bottom, then pour excess butter back into the cup, leaving the bottom lightly coated with sizzling butter. (If the butter doesn't sizzle, heat the pan longer before adding the batter.) Immediately ladle in a scant ⅓ cup of batter, tilt and swirl so it coats the bottom, and set the pan on the burner.

(recipe continues)

Lower the heat to medium, and cook the *palacinka* for a little less than a minute, until the underside is lightly browned in a lacy pattern. Flip it over with a spatula, and fry for 30 seconds or longer, until the second side is lightly browned, then remove it to a warm platter. Heat the empty pan briefly, then rapidly coat it with butter, fill it with batter, and cook another *palacinka*. Repeat the sequence, stacking up the finished *palacinke* on the platter, until all the batter is used up.

Fill and serve the *palacinke* as soon as possible, while fresh and warm. Keep the platter in a warm spot and cover the stack with a tent of foil or a large bowl turned upside down. Whip the heavy cream, unsweetened or with sugar to taste, to soft peaks.

Stir the melted chocolate, and reheat it if necessary so it is smooth and warm.

Take one *palacinka* off the stack and place it with its lacy-patterned side down. Spoon a generous tablespoon (or more) of warm chocolate in the center of the pancake, and spread it over the *palacinka*, leaving an inch-wide border uncoated. Scatter a spoonful of chopped walnuts on the chocolate layer, then fold the round in half, hiding the fillings, and fold again into a plump quarter-round.

Fill and fold all the *palacinke* the same way. For each serving, place two rounds, overlapping, on a dessert plate, heap some whipped cream on top, scatter some nuts on top of the cream, and drizzle warm chocolate in streaks and squiggles over the *palacinke* and the plate.

LIMONCELLO TIRAMISÙ

Tiramisù al Limoncello

One of the best things about tiramisù is its versatility: though the conventional version calls for espresso-soaked *savoiardi* (ladyfingers), I've found that other flavors can be incorporated into the dessert with great success. Here the brightness of fresh lemons and limoncello lace the cream and soaking syrup, resulting in a tiramisù that is refreshing and irresistible. Great for larger gatherings, it is always a dessert of choice at our house.

MAKES A 12- OR 13-INCH TIRAMISÙ,
SERVING 12 OR MORE

5 or 6 lemons

5 large eggs

1 cup sugar

1½ cups limoncello liqueur

1 cup water

1 pound (2 cups) mascarpone, at room temperature

40 ladyfingers (preferably imported Italian *savoiardi*),
or more as needed

Remove the zest of 2 or more of the lemons, using a fine grater, to get 2 tablespoons of zest. Squeeze out and strain the juice of these and the other lemons to get ¾ cup of fresh lemon juice.

Pour just enough water into a double-boiler pan so the water level is right below the bottom of the mixing bowl when it is sitting in the pan. Separate the eggs, putting yolks in the large bowl of the double boiler, and the whites in another stainless-steel bowl.

To make the base for the tiramisù: Heat the water in the pan to a steady simmer. Remove the top bowl from heat, and beat the egg yolks with ¼ cup of the sugar and ½ cup of the limoncello until well blended. Set the bowl over the simmering water, and whisk constantly, frequently scraping the whisk around the sides and bottom of the bowl, as the egg mixture expands and heats into a frothy sponge, 5 minutes or longer. When the sponge has thickened enough to form a ribbon when it drops on the surface, take the bowl off the double-boiler pan and let it cool.

Meanwhile, pour the remaining cup of limoncello, all of the lemon juice, the 1 cup water, and ½ cup of the sugar in a saucepan. Bring to a boil, stirring to dissolve the sugar, and cook for 5 minutes, evaporating the alcohol. Let the syrup cool completely.

In another large bowl, stir the mascarpone with a wooden spoon to soften it, then drop in the grated lemon zest and beat with a whisk until light and creamy. In another bowl, whip the egg whites with the remaining ¼ cup sugar until it holds moderately firm peaks.

When the cooked limoncello zabaglione is cooled,

(recipe continues)

scrape about a third of it over the mascarpone and fold it in with a large rubber spatula. Fold in the rest of the zabaglione in two or three additions. Now fold in the whipped egg whites in several additions, until the limoncello-mascarpone cream is light and evenly blended.

Pour some of the cooled syrup into a pan, no deeper than ¼ inch, to moisten the ladyfingers. One at a time, roll a ladyfinger in the syrup and quickly place it in a 9-by-13-inch Pyrex pan. Wet each cookie briefly—if it soaks up too much syrup, it will fall apart. Arrange the moistened ladyfingers in neat, tight rows in the pan, filling the bottom of the pan completely. You should be able to fit in about twenty ladyfingers in a single layer.

Scoop half of the limoncello-mascarpone cream onto the ladyfingers, and smooth it to fill the pan and cover them. Dip and arrange a second layer of ladyfingers in the pan, and cover it completely with the remainder of the cream.

Smooth the cream with the spatula, and seal the tiramisù airtight in plastic wrap. Before serving, refrigerate for 6 hours or up to 2 days, or put it in the freezer for 2 hours. To serve, cut portions of tiramisù in any size you like, and lift them out of the pan onto dessert plates.

CHOCOLATE BREAD PARFAIT

Pane di Cioccolato al Cucchiaio

This dessert recalls for me the chocolate-and-bread sandwiches that were sometimes my lunch, and always a special treat. How simple but how delicious those two pieces of bread with chocolate in between were. This is another inventive way to recycle leftover bread as the foundation of an elegant layered dessert. Though it is soaked with chocolate-and-espresso sauce and buried in whipped cream, the bread doesn't disintegrate, and provides a great textural contrast in every heavenly spoonful. Even when you think you have nothing in the house for dessert, this is a recipe I am sure you can conjure up. It is best when served immediately, while the melted chocolate is still warm and runny.

SERVES 6

8 ounces bittersweet or semisweet chocolate, finely chopped

8 ounces country-style white bread, crusts removed

½ cup freshly brewed espresso

2 tablespoons dark rum

2 tablespoons sugar

1½ cups heavy cream, chilled

1 cup sliced almonds, toasted

Put the chopped chocolate in a bowl set in a pan of hot (not boiling) water. When the chocolate begins to melt, stir until completely smooth. Keep it warm, over the water, off the heat.

Slice the bread into ½-inch-thick slices, and lay them flat in one layer, close together, on a tray or baking sheet.

Pour the warm espresso into a spouted measuring cup, stir in the rum and sugar until the sugar dissolves, and stir in half the melted chocolate. Pour the coffee-rum-chocolate sauce all over the bread slices, then flip them over and turn them on the tray, to make sure all the surfaces are coated. Let the bread absorb the sauce for a few minutes.

Meanwhile, whip the cream until soft peaks form.

To assemble the parfaits: Break the soaked bread into 1-inch pieces. Use half the pieces to make the bottom parfait layer in six serving glasses, dropping an equal amount of chocolate-dipped bread into each. Scrape up some of the unabsorbed chocolate sauce that remains on the baking sheet, and drizzle a bit over the bread layers. Drizzle some of the remaining melted chocolate as well. Next, drop a layer of whipped cream into the glasses, using up half the cream. Top the cream layer with toasted almonds, using half the nuts. Repeat with another layer of all ingredients. To finish, dollop another layer of whipped cream, using it all up, and sprinkle on the remaining almonds and drizzle remaining melted chocolate on top of each parfait.

RICOTTA COOKIES

Biscotti di Ricotta

I love ricotta almost anywhere, but in particular in these moist and delicious cookies. I know my mother will be ready to eat some as well—ricotta is her favorite by far. Adding ricotta to baked goods lightens up the dessert and adds the complexity of the sweet milk curds to the final flavors.

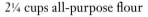 **MAKES ABOUT 3½ DOZEN COOKIES**

2¼ cups all-purpose flour

1 teaspoon baking powder

Pinch of kosher salt

1 cup granulated sugar

½ cup (1 stick) butter, at room temperature

2 large eggs

8 ounces fresh ricotta, drained

½ teaspoon vanilla extract

Zest of 1 lemon, finely grated, plus ¼ cup freshly squeezed lemon juice

2 cups confectioners' sugar, sifted

Preheat oven to 325 degrees F. Sift together flour, baking powder, and salt into a bowl, and set aside. Line two cookie pans with parchment paper.

Cream the granulated sugar and butter in a mixer fitted with the paddle attachment at high speed until light and fluffy, about 2 minutes. Reduce the speed to medium, and crack in the eggs one at a time, beating well in between additions. Plop in the ricotta, vanilla, and lemon zest, and beat to combine. Add the flour mixture and beat at low speed until just combined; do not overmix.

Drop the dough in heaping tablespoons onto the sheet pans. Place in oven and bake, rotating pans halfway through the baking time, until the cookies are puffed, golden, and cooked all the way through, about 20 to 22 minutes. Remove, and cool on wire racks.

When the cookies are completely cool, make the glaze. In a bowl, whisk together the confectioners' sugar and lemon juice to make a smooth glaze. Adjust the consistency with a little water or more confectioners' sugar to make a glaze thick enough to stick to the cookies when dipped. Dip the tops of the cookies in the glaze, and let dry on racks.

ALMOND TORTA WITH CHOCOLATE CHIPS

Torta di Mandorle con Gocce di Cioccolato

I must say that my original recipe was for plain almond cake, which is a favorite at our house, but here I add chocolate chips. Who doesn't like chocolate chips? You can also substitute dried cranberries, dried cherries, or currants in this delicious basic recipe. This is particularly good accompanied by whipped cream, ice cream, or zabaglione. I adapted it from one favorite to another—so, really, it's the perfect dish to close this collection.

MAKES A 10-INCH CAKE, SERVING 10 OR MORE

1¾ cups all-purpose flour, plus more for the pan

½ teaspoon baking powder

¼ teaspoon kosher salt

10 ounces (2½ sticks) butter, softened, plus more for the pan

1 cup sugar

5 large eggs

Zest of 1 lemon, finely grated (about 2 teaspoons)

1 teaspoon pure almond extract

2 cups almond flour or almond meal

1 cup semisweet chocolate chips

½ cup sliced blanched almonds, lightly toasted

Confectioners' sugar, for dusting

Arrange a rack in the center of the oven, and heat to 350 degrees F.

Sift together the all-purpose flour, baking powder, and salt. Cream the butter and sugar in a mixer at medium-high speed until light and fluffy, about 2 minutes. Beat in the eggs, one at a time. Beat in the lemon zest and almond extract, then raise the speed to high and beat the batter until very light, a minute or more. At low speed, mix in half of the sifted flour mixture, beating just until it is incorporated; beat in half the almond flour. Scrape the bowl, and mix in the remaining all-purpose flour and remaining almond flour. Beat briefly at medium speed to a smooth batter, then, again on low speed, mix in the chocolate chips, just until evenly distributed.

Scrape the batter into a buttered and floured 10-inch springform pan, and spread it in an even layer. Scatter the sliced almonds all over the top.

Bake the torta for 45 minutes—rotating the pan halfway through the baking time—or until the cake is golden brown on top and a knife inserted in the center comes out clean. Cool the cake in the pan for about 10 minutes on a wire rack. Run the blade of a paring knife around the edge of the cake, then open the spring and remove the side ring.

Cool the cake completely before serving. Cut it into wedges, and dust with confectioners' sugar.

Index

Page references in *italic* refer to illustrations.

A Note About the Authors

Lidia Matticchio Bastianich was born in Pula, Istria, and came to the United States in 1958. She opened her first restaurant, Buonavia, in Queens, in 1971 and a second restaurant, Villa Secondo, shortly thereafter. Their tremendous success inspired her to launch Felidia in 1981 in Manhattan, followed by Becco, Esca, Del Posto, and Eataly (also in New York), and Lidia's in Kansas City and Pittsburgh. She has developed a line of Lidia's Pasta and Lidia's Sauces, available across the United States.

Lidia Bastianich is the author of eight previous books: *La Cucina di Lidia, Lidia's Italian Table, Lidia's Italian-American Kitchen, Lidia's Family Table, Lidia's Italy, Lidia Cooks from the Heart of Italy*, and *Lidia's Italy in America* (the last three with Tanya Bastianich Manuali) and her children's book, *Nonna Tell Me a Story*. She has also been the host of several public-television series—*Lidia's Italian Table, Lidia's Italian-American Kitchen, Lidia's Family Table, Lidia's Italy, Lidia's Italy in America*, and *Lidia Celebrates America*—and she gives lectures on Italian cuisine across the country. Lidia also has developed a very interactive website, www.lidiasitaly.com, where she shares daily recipes, pictures, information about seasonal products, tips, and personal stories. She lives on Long Island.

Tanya Bastianich Manuali's visits to Italy as a child sparked her passion for the country's art and culture. She dedicated herself to the study of Italian Renaissance art during her college years at Georgetown and earned a master's degree from Syracuse University and a doctorate from Oxford University. Living and studying in many regions of Italy for seven years, she taught art history to American students in Florence, and also met her husband, Corrado Manuali, from Rome. Tanya co-created, with Shelly Burgess Nicotra, Esperienze Italiane, a custom-tour company devoted to the discovery of Italian food, wine, and art. Tanya is integrally involved in the production of Lidia's public-television series and is active daily in the family restaurant business. She has also led the development of the website, www.lidiasitaly.com, and related publications and merchandise lines for tabletop and cooking. Tanya has co-authored three previous books with her mother: *Lidia's Italy, Lidia Cooks from the Heart of Italy*, and *Lidia's Italy in America*. In 2010, Tanya co-authored *Reflections of the Breast: Breast Cancer in Art Through the Ages*, a social-art-historical look at breast cancer in art from Ancient Egypt to today. Tanya and Corrado live in New York City with their children, Lorenzo and Julia.